SEATTLE'S WATERFRONT
THE WALKER'S GUIDE TO THE HISTORY OF ELLIOTT BAY

Marc J. Hershman, Susan Heikkala and Caroline Tobin

Prepared at the Institute for Marine Studies
University of Washington

Waterfront Awareness, Seattle

Waterfront Awareness . . .
a nonprofit corporation dedicated to building understanding and affection for the urban waterfront.

©1981 by Waterfront Awareness
All rights reserved

Published in the United States by Waterfront Awareness
2342 Thirty-Fourth Avenue S.
Seattle, Washington 98144

Distributed by University of Washington Press
4045 Brooklyn Avenue N.E.
Seattle, Washington 98105

Printed in the United States of America

Design: Wilkins & Peterson, Rick Lindberg

Library of Congress Cataloging in Publication Data
Hershman, Marc, 1942-
   Seattle's waterfront.
   Bibliography: p.
   Includes index.
   1. Seattle (Wash.—
Harbor—History. 2. Waterfronts—Washington (State)—
Seattle—History. 3. Merchant marine—Washington (State)—
Seattle—History. 4. Seattle (Wash.)—Description—Guidebooks. I. Heikkala, Susan. II. Tobin, Caroline. III. University of Washington. Institute for Marine Studies. IV. Title.
HE554.SS5H47   387.1'09797'77
81-51936
ISBN 0-295-95852-9 (pbk.)
AACR2

Marc J. Hershman is Associate Professor of Marine Studies and Adjunct Professor of Law at the University of Washington. He is program manager for Coastal Resources at the University's Institute for Marine Studies. He is also editor-in-chief of the *Coastal Zone Management Journal.*

Susan Heikkala is a planner and urban designer. She is currently a Research Associate with the College of Architecture and Urban Planning at the University of Washington.

Caroline Tobin is a community planner for Vashon Island with the King County Planning Division, and she has written previously about Seattle's central waterfront.

CONTENTS

ACKNOWLEDGMENTS

This project has been funded with the assistance of a matching grant-in-aid from the National Trust for Historic Preservation made possible by the U.S. Department of the Interior, under the provisions of the National Historic Preservation Act of 1966.

Substantial funding was also provided by the Washington Sea Grant Program, through grant number NA-81AA-D-00030 from the National Oceanic and Atmospheric Administration.

In addition, we gratefully acknowledge the following organizations for providing further support for this project: Institute for Marine Studies, University of Washington; City of Seattle with Coastal Zone Management funds from the Washington State Department of Ecology; Port of Seattle; Puget Sound Maritime Historical Society; Propeller Club of the Port of Seattle; and Washington State Department of Natural Resources.

There have also been numerous groups and individuals who have given generously of their time and ideas in the preparation of this historical guidebook. We have relied on experts on particular aspects of Elliott Bay. Special thanks are due to members of our advisory committee who provided the initial direction for the guidebook and who reviewed several drafts. In particular, we appreciate the efforts of Jack Dillon, maritime historian and member of the Puget Sound Maritime Historical Society, who has been an enthusiastic supporter and a painstaking reviewer. We also wish to thank Rosemary Horwood for her continuing encouragement and support and the Puget Sound Maritime Historical Society for donation of numerous photographs from their Williamson Collection.

We wish especially to thank Melissa Rohan, executive director of Waterfront Awareness; Patricia Silver, our editor; Gina Artus for research assistance; and Natala Reyburn for her careful typing of numerous drafts. We are also grateful to Vivian Bowden whose earlier research for the *Elliott Bay: Your Waterfront* exhibit and brochure expedited the research for this book. Finally, we wish to thank the many people who we interviewed and who reviewed drafts of this book.

FOREWORD

Seattle is a maritime city. It began in 1852 when the area's first pioneers paddled their canoes around the entire perimeter of Elliott Bay seeking protected, deep water, which their campsite on Alki Point did not have. They found it in the area that is now the foot of Yesler Way, and when Henry Yesler built his sawmill and wharf there the dreamed-of city was on its way.

A rich maritime history lives on along the Seattle waterfront. The essence of that heritage is captured in the stories of waterfront people and their enterprise, tales of wooden steamers and Gold Rush fever, of shipbuilding and container cranes. These stories of past events on Elliott Bay show the vital role the waterfront has played in Seattle's history, shaping the city we know today.

Although the city has become the center of a great metropolitan area, comparatively few people show interest in its maritime heritage. The magazine *Sea Chest*, published quarterly by the Puget Sound Maritime Historical Society, has small circulation outside the Society, and the Maritime Wing at the Museum of History and Industry is never crowded.

Some excellent historians and writers have contributed to the lore of Seattle's maritime heritage, but general public awareness still seems limited. One purpose of this book is to heighten public interest in this fascinating subject — and the central waterfront of Seattle is the place to begin. Millions of people pass through or visit the waterfront each year. The central waterfront can become a center for interpreting the city's history and its maritime affairs, linking the present to the past by pointing out remnants that illustrate the evolution of shoreside facilities.

Enjoy what follows.

D. E. (Ned) Skinner
President
The Skinner Corporation

6

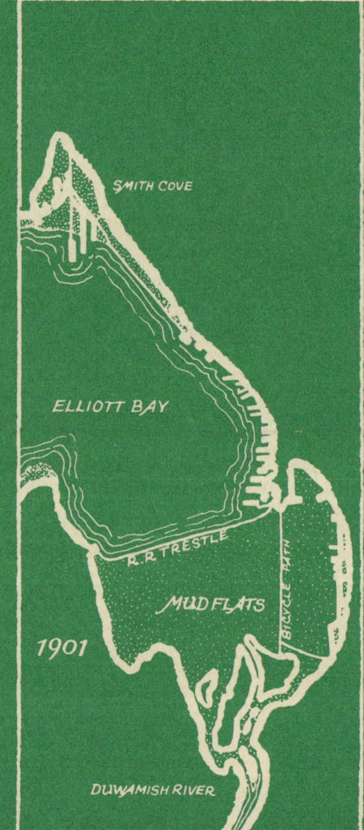

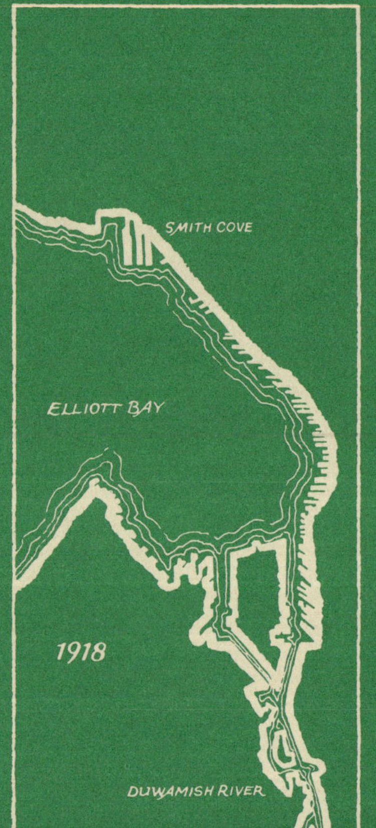

The Changing Shape of Elliott Bay

The Leading Edge of a Changing City

"To know Seattle one must know its waterfront." This simple phrase captures the essence of the waterfront's importance to the city; an understanding of Seattle's heritage must begin on Elliott Bay, where individuals and industries have continually provided the spark for the city's growth. Seattle was born on the waterfront, where the city's first sawmills were built and where most of the Puget Sound steamers were based. The railroads were drawn to the busy harbor, and the shipyards have produced ships by the thousands. Seattle's ties to Alaska and the Orient were forged on the waterfront. Elliott Bay also became the hub of a vast network of travel and recreation. This dynamic history is reflected in the diversity of the waterfront today. In short, the waterfront is Seattle's leading edge.

This wide variety of activity has been drawn to the Elliott Bay shoreline by the natural amenities of the area. Its rich wildlife resources, both on the shore and in the water, drew the Indian people there for winter camps. The pioneers, in turn, were attracted to the area by this abundance as well as by the deep, protected harbor, with its promise of future trade and industry. The harbor has also beckoned people to its shores for relaxation — the bay has been host to pleasure boats and waterfront strollers alike. Trade, industry, and recreation are big business on the waterfront today, providing work for about 12,000 people and relaxation for far more.

The natural features of Elliott Bay have also proved adaptable to changing needs. Seattle's shoreline has been reshaped several times to accommodate pressures from the expanding city and from the physical demands of new freight-handling techniques. The shoreline is as malleable as a block of clay, being washed down and built out to fit the needs of the growing community. In the earliest days of the pioneers, sawmills, ships, and sailboats crowded together on the central waterfront, but later they began to spread out along the harbor, shifting north, south, and toward West Seattle on new land created out of tideflats.

The visitor to today's central waterfront can see the vestiges of bygone days and visit sites where the colorful events in Seattle's past took place. The stories of eras, events, and people which follow are pieces of the complex fabric of the waterfront's history, and they are an essential key to the city's heritage. The central waterfront is a living museum, free to all, retelling the story of the four major eras of Seattle's growth.

The story begins with the *Indian and Pioneer Era*, from the days when the Indians were the only people on the shores of Elliott Bay, through the year 1851 when the first white settlers arrived, to 1889 when the Great Fire leveled much of the young city's downtown. Through these years, Seattle was carved out of the wilderness, and the population grew to about 27,000. Much of the city's waterfront character was formed at this time as the early settlers worked hard to make Seattle attractive to business and livable for their families. By the end of this era, Seattle was no longer a rough-and-tumble frontier town, but a prosperous, young city with streetcar lines, a municipal water system, police and fire protection, numerous civic organizations, and a thriving waterfront that included sawmills, coal bunkers, grist mills, steamboats, and railroads. In those early years, nearly everything in Seattle happened on the waterfront.

The *Waterfront Heyday Era*, from 1890 to 1920, was one of phenomenal growth. During the first decade of this era, Seattle boomed and the waterfront led the way. The Great Northern Railroad brought Seattle its first transcontinental link in 1893 when it located on the waterfront and launched an era of unprecedented trade growth. To make room for new industries, the tideflats were reclaimed in the south bay starting in 1895. A lucrative Far East trade began in 1896 when the Japanese ship *Miike Maru* docked in Elliott Bay. In 1897 the arrival of the S.S. *Portland* with its famous "ton of gold" from Alaska's Klondike kicked off a huge economic boom in shipbuilding and provisioning for the Alaska trade.

During this era, a "can-do" attitude prevailed. No job was too large for the citizens of Seattle— entire hills were leveled and moved to fill the tideflats, and in just one year the piers were all rebuilt to serve burgeoning trade.

Rapid growth continued through World War I, and Seattle became a city with a population of about 315,000, dominated by the tallest building west of the Mississippi, the Smith Tower built in 1914. The shape of the waterfront changed radically during this era as it became a crossroads for steamers, trains, motor vehicles, and people.

With the end of World War I and the beginning of a post-war depression, the waterfront entered an *Era of Uncertainty* marked by the ups and downs of marine trade and industry. This spanned the years from 1920 to 1960, during which time there was a major shift from marine to rail and truck transport on Puget Sound and the West Coast. The waterfront was at its lowest point during the Great Depression of the 1930s which was followed by labor unrest, deeply affecting Seattle's shipbuilding and maritime commerce.

World War II brought a new surge of shipbuilding and wartime-related commerce, but this was short-lived. Boeing aircraft corporation was now in the industrial limelight, and the central waterfront was especially hard hit. The piers

Take a Historic Walk along the Waterfront

The chapters of this book and the Guidemap relate to the central waterfront of Seattle— the well-traveled area from Piers 48 to 70. Other parts of Elliott Bay are sometimes noted as well, such as the area north of Pier 71 where there are additional parks and port facilities, and the industrialized south bay, where much of the marine commerce of the city now takes place.

Take a tour along the central waterfront using the Guidemap and referring to the text for more detail, or read the book at home or over some fish and chips at a shoreside restaurant before taking a waterfront stroll. Or read it just for fun!

A Guide to Pier Numbering

Yesler's Wharf, Colman Dock, Pier A, Pier 3, Pier 70. For many, this history of the waterfront will contain a confusing array of names and numbers associated with the piers, because over the years the pier-identification system has changed radically several times. Originally, the wharves were given names, usually commemorating the individual builder or the company that built them, such as Yesler's Wharf or Colman Dock. The random naming of piers continued until 1901.

Along with a massive rebuilding of the waterfront, R.H. Thomson, Seattle's celebrated city engineer, established a new pier-identification system. Moving north from Yesler Way, the piers were numbered consecutively—Pier 1, Pier 2, and so forth. South of

Seattle's waterfront, 1878.

there were too small for
many of the ships and in-
dustries. Businesses moved
to the south harbor or to
Smith Cove to occupy
modern facilities. Obsoles-
cence and blight, vacancy
and decay, characterized
much of the central waterfront during this era.
Its function and place in
a busy harbor were no
longer clear.

A new direction was
charted in the early 1960s in
conjunction with the revitali-
zation of all of downtown, and
a remarkable transformation
began that endures today.
This is the *Waterfront
Revival Era*, both for maritime trade and for waterfront
recreation. A major face
lifting of the commercial
waterfront in the south harbor and Smith Cove area has
been spurred on by new and
specialized forms of cargo
handling, such as contain-

erization and bulk-cargo-
handling systems. Seattle is
now one of the most active
ports on the West Coast and
one of the leaders in modern
port technology and
management. Paralleling
this change has been the
revival of the central waterfront, a conversion of
the functionally obsolete
and decaying piers into a
major leisure center for the
city and region. The past
twenty years have seen
Elliott Bay and its shoreline
make an about-face from
languor and decadence
toward vibrance and ex-
citement in trade, industry,
and recreation.

The waterfront is one of
Seattle's greatest assets.
Whether its worth is mea-
sured by value of cargo or
days of recreation enjoyed,
it is Seattle's lifeblood. The
stories that follow explore
some of the countless ways

Ship chandler on Colman Dock.

Yesler, the piers were
given a letter designation
starting with Pier A at
the foot of Washington
Street. Although the
piers were still known by
their names, most of
them now also had a
permanent letter or
number designation.

This system was not
foolproof, however. For
example, Colman Dock,
situated between Piers 2
and 3, was never as-
signed a number. The
apparent reason is that
the Northern Pacific Railroad built the piers sur-
rounding Colman Dock,
but labeled only the piers
they owned and not the
intervening one.

Thomson's system
rapidly became unwork-
able. Duplication of
numbers resulted in a
ship's docking at Pier 42,
or Smith Cove Pier, while
longshoremen stood
waiting for its arrival at
an entirely different Pier
42 on the central water-

front. In 1944 the U.S. government, which was directing all wartime harbor traffic, finally re-numbered the piers to eliminate the perennial confusion, using a system still followed today. Beginning in West Seattle, the piers were numbered consecutively, leaving gaps in the sequence if no pier existed and if there was room for one to be built. Thus today, the pier following Pier 71 is Pier 86, in recognition of the possibility of future pier development in the mile of open waterfront between them.

the central waterfront and Elliott Bay have been used and how Seattle's leaders have molded it over the years. They emphasize the bay's history as a physical resource and the central role of the waterfront in the city's evolution from wilderness to major metropolitan center. These stories hint at others, which are reserved for a later telling—stories about the labor movement, steamboat companies, tugboats, the fishing industry, or Seattle's rich natural environment. The chapters that follow describe Seattle's *maritime* heritage—the changing use and form of the waterfront over the span of 130 years—and how that reflects the energy and enterprise of the people who have led Seattle to its preeminent position in the Pacific Northwest.

Pier 62, about 1920.

Puget Sound Maritime Historical Society, Williamson Collection

MAJOR WATERFRONT ERAS

INDIAN AND PIONEER ERA

WATERFRONT HEYDAY ERA

1850 1860 1870 1880 1890 1900

EVENTS ON SEATTLE'S WATERFRONT

1852 Denny party lands in Elliott Bay
1853 Beginning of Mosquito Fleet
1854 Yesler's Wharf built
1856 Battle of Seattle/*U.S.S. Decatur* in harbor
1865 Seattle incorporates
1868 First ship to Alaska
1869 Seattle incorporates a second time
1875 Seattle and Walla Walla R.R. complete to Renton
1880's City emerges—Spring Hill Water Co., telephone exchange
1886 Anti-Chinese riots
1888 Electric railway
1889 Great Seattle Fire
1893 Northern Pacific R.R. to Seattle
1895 Tideland filling begins
1896 *Miike Maru* opens Orient trade
1897 *S.S. Portland* arrives with "Ton of Gold"
1898 Morans build 12 boats for Yukon trade
1904 Nebraska completed
1905 R.R. Tunnel completed

MOSQUITO FLEET

SHIPBUILDING

GENERAL COMMERCE

RAILROADS

IMPORTANT REGIONAL AND NATIONAL EVENTS

1850's California Gold Rush
1854 Trade opens with Japan
1861-65 Civil War
1867 Alaska purchased from Russia
1873 Economic depression/Tacoma is Northern Pacific R.R. terminus
1877 First cannery on Puget Sound
1882 Chinese Exclusion Act
1889 Washington enters union
1893 Financial panic
1896 Klondike Gold Rush begins
1898 Spanish American War
Gas powered engines in use
1914 Panama Canal opens
Airplane travel
1916 Prohibition begins

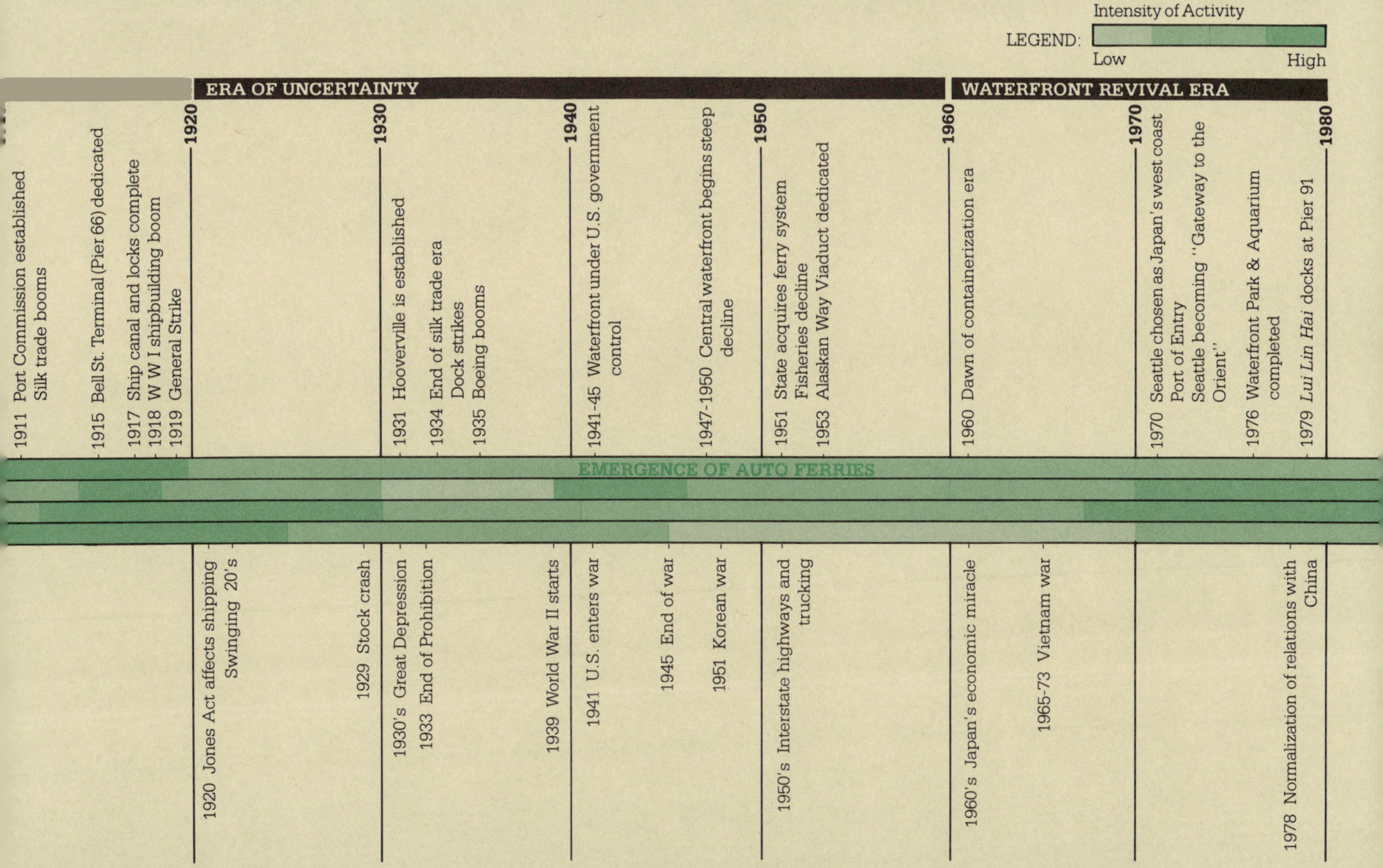

Intensity of Activity

LEGEND:
Low   High

ERA OF UNCERTAINTY   WATERFRONT REVIVAL ERA

1920   **1930**   **1940**   **1950**   **1960**   **1970**   **1980**

1911 Port Commission established
      Silk trade booms
1915 Bell St. Terminal (Pier 66) dedicated
1917 Ship canal and locks complete
1918 W W I shipbuilding boom
1919 General Strike
1931 Hooverville is established
1934 End of silk trade era
      Dock strikes
1935 Boeing booms
1941-45 Waterfront under U.S. government control
1947-1950 Central waterfront begins steep decline
1951 State acquires ferry system
      Fisheries decline
1953 Alaskan Way Viaduct dedicated
1960 Dawn of containerization era
1970 Seattle chosen as Japan's west coast Port of Entry
      Seattle becoming "Gateway to the Orient"
1976 Waterfront Park & Aquarium completed
1979 *Lui Lin Hai* docks at Pier 91

EMERGENCE OF AUTO FERRIES

1920 Jones Act affects shipping
      Swinging 20's
1929 Stock crash
1930's Great Depression
1933 End of Prohibition
1939 World War II starts
1941 U.S. enters war
1945 End of war
1951 Korean war
1950's Interstate highways and trucking
1960's Japan's economic miracle
1965-73 Vietnam war
1978 Normalization of relations with China

Indian Salmon Weir

First to Settle on Elliott Bay

Long before the pioneers set foot on the shores of Elliott Bay, the Duwamish Indian people had a winter village there known as Djidjila'letch (djee-djee-lah-letch) or "little crossing over place." It was located near what is now First Avenue and Yesler Way in Pioneer Square, and its name referred to a path that crossed the low isthmus there, connecting a peninsula to the south with higher ground to the north.

The name Duwamish, meaning "inside people," describes the area where they lived inside the Duwamish River and along Elliott Bay. Most of the other tribes lived on less protected harbors on Puget Sound. Djidjila'letch was one of the largest villages of the Duwamish people because of its location at the starting point of a trail that connected Elliott Bay with Lake Washington, the villages near Renton, and Yakima and Snoqualmie passes.[1] Djidjila'letch is said to have included eight large longhouses, the traditional, cedar-planked houses of the Duwamish people. As many as 200 may have lived in these houses, probably before 1800. When Arthur Denny, William Bell, and Carson Boren first crossed over from Alki Point early in 1852, they found only the remains of one longhouse; the village had been deserted.

The Duwamish Indian people depended upon the diverse and abundant resources of Elliott Bay and the Duwamish River. Like other coastal tribes, they were primarily a fishing culture. Their favorite fish was salmon, which they often caught in tripod weirs built across the Duwamish River upstream from its mouth. As the salmon migrated upstream, they were held back by the fence, picked up from the traps with nets, and clubbed. The Indian people viewed the annual return of the salmon as a miraculous event. According to their beliefs, the fish were immortal beings who sacrificed their bodies for man's benefit.[2]

The Duwamish also turned to the waterfront as a location for their sweat lodges. Between what are today Yesler Way and Columbia Street, they built small huts of boards and wreckage from the beach. Heated stones were placed inside the huts and then drenched with water. After spreading green branches on the stones, the Duwamish again covered them with water. They believed that sweating cleansed both the body and the spirit. From the lodges, they jumped into Elliott Bay and rubbed themselves with twigs.[3]

From the time the *Exact* brought the first white settlers to Alki Point in 1851, however, the Duwamish people's days as premier inhabitants of Elliott Bay were numbered. They lost most of their land in the Point Elliott Treaty of 1855 in exchange for shared space on a reservation on Bainbridge Island. In 1856 the Battle of Seattle took place, spurred on by the Klickitat Indians from eastern Washington. It was the only major battle between the Indian people and the white settlers, and the outcome of this skirmish was determined on the waterfront. The presence of the sloop of war, the U.S.S. *Decatur,* tipped the scale in favor of the settlers and gave them the final victory.

Thereafter the Indian people mingled with the white settlers and continued to camp along the waterfront. During the 1880s and 1890s, they camped on Ballast Island at the foot of Washington Street by the entrance to Ocean Dock, approximately where First Avenue and Washington Street intersect today. Ballast Island was a raised mound produced over the years by material dumped from ships, and the Indian people were allowed to camp there because the area was not immediately suitable for construction.[1] Another camp known as Ba'qbaqwab (bak-bak-wab) was located at the foot of Bell Street, near where the Port of Seattle's headquarters are now. The name, meaning "little prairies," was given to the waterfront camp even though the prairies were actually

In the 1880s the Indian people camped at Ba'qbaqwab, near today's Pier 66.

Historical Society of Seattle and King County

above the beach, near present-day Seattle Center.

After the Point Elliott Treaty, the Duwamish camped close to the settlers along the early waterfront because they wished to remain near their traditional hunting and fishing grounds, and they had also come to depend upon the white economy for survival. They picked hops, worked at Henry Yesler's sawmill, and traded with the settlers. A common scene in the early fall was a line of canoes entering the harbor on the way to or from the hop fields in North Bend, Issaquah, and the White River Valley. The Indian people sold baskets, moccasins, and clams along the sidewalks and peddled fish, shellfish, and berries from house to house. In an effort to curtail this activity, one of the city's first five

The Battle of Seattle

The settlers defeated the Indian people on January 26, 1856, primarily because of the sloop of war, the U.S.S. *Decatur*, which had come to Puget Sound in 1855 to protect the settlers. At the time of the skirmish, the *Decatur* was anchored in Elliott Bay to be repaired and to assist Seattle in the event of an attack. Because of rumors of a forthcoming offensive, Seattle citizens had constructed blockhouses and a stockade late in 1855. The reason behind the attack was the recent treaties which had given the settlers land that had belonged to the Indian people. The day before the outbreak, Isaac Stevens, the first governor of Washington Territory, had assured the settlers that Seattle was as safe as New York or

San Francisco.

On the night of January 25, however, friendly Indians warned the pioneers of an impending attack, spurred on by the Klickitats from eastern Washington. Fighting broke out early on the morning of January 26. By ten o'clock that evening, the Indians had retreated into the darkness toward Lake Washington, driven back by gunfire from the cannon on board the *Decatur* and the ship's howitzer, which had been set up on shore.

The settlers took precautions against future trouble by building a new fortification, a five-foot-high barricade around the town, with lumber donated by Henry Yesler, but Seattle never faced another attack.

Painting of the 1856 Battle of Seattle by Emily Inez Denny.

Ballast Island, Indian camping ground in the 1880s and 1890s.

18

How Seattle Got Its Name

In 1853 the town that was growing on the shores of Elliott Bay was named for Chief Sealth, friend to Doc Maynard and Arthur Denny and leader of the Duwamish Indian people. Seattle is the anglicized version of Sealth, and there is some indication that Sealth did not feel honored that the town was given his name. According to the tradition of Sealth's people, the name was the property of the family. Someone else wanting to use it was required to give some form of payment in exchange for the use of the name. Chief Sealth may have also been unhappy with the choice of his name because the Indian people believed that the mention of a dead person's name disturbs the spirit, which then tries to return to earth.[1]

Chief Sealth.

ordinances, published in the *Seattle Gazette* on February 7, 1865, limited the Indian people's movement around the city.[5]

Eventually, as buildings were constructed around the turn of the century on landfill areas like Ballast Island, the white culture overran that of the Indian people, and all traces of the camps along the central waterfront disappeared. Today the Duwamish maintain a tribal office south of Seattle in Burien, but they have never had their own reservation and have not been recognized by the U.S. government as an official tribe.[6] Near the Port of Seattle's Terminal 107 off West Marginal Way is the site of an archaeological dig. This site, several miles south of the central waterfront, is the only tangible remnant of the Duwamish culture that once thrived along Elliott Bay.

Today the spirit of the Indian people lives on along the Elliott Bay waterfront, even though few traces of their culture remain. That spirit was perhaps best expressed by Chief Sealth, for whom Seattle is named.

Every part of this soil is sacred in the estimation of my people. Every hillside, every valley, every plain and grove has been hallowed by some sad or happy event in days long vanished. Even the rocks, which seem to be dumb and dead as they swelter in the sun along the silent shore, thrill with the memories of stirring events connected with the lives of my people, and the very dust upon which you now stand responds more lovingly to their footsteps than to yours, because it is rich with the blood of our ancestors and our bare feet are conscious of the sympathetic touch...

And when the last Red Man shall have perished, and the memory of my tribe shall have become a myth among the White Men, these shores will swarm with the invisible dead of my tribe, and when your children's children think themselves alone in the field, the store, the shop, upon the highway, or in the silence of the pathless woods, they will not be alone. In all the earth there is no place dedicated to solitude. At night when the streets of your cities and villages are silent and you think them deserted, they will throng with the returning hosts that once filled them and still love this beautiful land. The White Man will never be alone.[7]

TIDEFLATS TO MODERN HARBOR
LAKE UNION
1916
1920
1929
1903
1936
1908
1917
1910
ELLIOTT BAY
1910
1895
1902
LAKE WASHINGTON
1910
1918
1921
1916
1914
DUWAMISH RIVER
Major Landfills and Regrades

Shaping Seattle's Waterfront

In 1856 a view of Elliott Bay's shore encompassed densely forested hills above extensive tideflats, salt marshes, and gravel beaches ringing a protected harbor about two miles wide and six miles long. Swimming and clam digging were the only things to do west of Commercial Street, or what is now First Avenue South, since today's shoreline was at that time under thirty to forty feet of water at high tide.[1] Water lapped the shore between present-day Alaskan Way and First Avenue, and a small peninsula of dry land extended only as far south as Jackson Street. The neck of the peninsula, near the pergola in today's Pioneer Square, was submerged at high tide, leaving only a small island of about seven or eight acres.

Travel south from what is today Yesler Way required a boat since the mouth of the Duwamish River was a 2,100-acre tideflat, and even then it was necessary to keep an eye on the tides or risk being stranded on a bed of ooze, waiting for hours for the tide to turn. Directly to the east and north of the shore were forested hillsides and, in some areas, steep bluffs. A portion of the old shore bluff is still visible beneath the viaduct east of Piers 62 and 63. This bluff climbed gradually from today's Pioneer Square area to Pike Street, where a 100-foot cliff dropped to the beach. Only a ravine in the vicinity of Seneca Street interrupted the steady, uphill progression.[2]

Seattle's shoreline has had a radical face lifting since those days. Now the city has a "made" waterfront. As have many modern coastal cities, Seattle has sculpted and reshaped the original shoreline in order to promote trade and to develop a thriving port and city. In the space of only eighty years, "the contour of the harbor was changed, a whole new waterfront was lifted up and added to the city, hills were washed down, a river bed was straightened, lakes once separated were joined and hundreds of acres of building sites were either dumped in by carload or pumped out of the water."[3] Some systematic digging in the vicinity of Yesler Way and Washington Street today would undoubtedly unearth many remnants of Seattle's past—remains of the old Duwamish Indian village, Djidjila'letch; sawdust and slabs from Henry Yesler's sawmill; and rock ballast from old schooners.

It was Henry Yesler who first used waterfront landfill as a means of moving the shoreline. His sawmill was located at the foot of Mill Street, now Yesler Way, on the neck of the low-lying peninsula that was regularly inundated by the tides. Although at first he burned the slabs and wastes from his mill, he soon began to dump them instead as fill around the isthmus and at the foot of his wharf. Because of Yesler's efforts, Seattle's first landfill became known as "The Sawdust," and, after years of continued filling, Yesler's Wharf was said to weigh several hundred thousand tons. The achievement became an inspiration for future earth-moving projects. As early as 1875, the *Daily Pacific Tribune* reported that "to a certain degree he [had] solved the question of the practicability of filling in the mud flats, and creating room for transaction of the heavy business of the city of Seattle."[4]

Seattle's early commerce provided another source of landfill along the waterfront. Tons of rock ballast were dumped at the ends of the piers from the holds of trading ships to make room for Washington's lumber and coal. California was Seattle's first trading partner, and forty thousand tons of San Francisco's Telegraph Hill lie buried under Washington Street, the site of one of the first commercial docks. In fact, the waterfront fill has even more cosmopolitan origins—ballast from Liverpool, Boston, New York, Valparaiso, Mazatlán, Honolulu, Hong Kong, Sydney, and Melbourne lies buried beneath the old wharves.[5] As a result of this continual dumping, Ballast Island rose from the depths at the foot of Washington Street by the entrance to Ocean Dock inland from where the Public Boat

Landing is today.

The natural shoreline contours were modified still more as railroad rights of way, streets, and piers began to be built on pilings in Elliott Bay south of Yesler's Wharf in order to compensate for a shortage of level waterfront land and to provide additional wharf space. The trestles built in 1875 for the city's first railroad, the Seattle and Walla Walla, ran from the coal bunkers at the foot of King Street directly through the tideflats to Renton. In 1882 Commercial Street was ex-

Sunken Ships along Seattle's Waterfront

Rock ballast is not all that Seattle's commerce has provided for landfill materials. At least two ships, the bark *Windward* and the sidewheel steamer *Idaho,* are forever embedded in the waterfront under years of accumulated fill, and a third came close to the same fate.

In 1875 James Colman, who at that time ran Yesler's sawmill, bought the wreck of the *Windward,* which had gone aground one foggy December day in Useless Bay on Whidbey Island. He had it towed to Seattle and left it on the beach between Columbia and Marion streets to salvage the metal off the old ship. Some say he also lived on board while he ran the mill. The *Windward* never moved again, and in 1885 the Seattle, Lake

Shore, and Eastern line built its railroad over it, driving the trestle pilings through the hull of the old ship. In 1889, after the Great Fire, the mill operator rebuilt the Colman Building next to the remains of the ship that was once his home. Today the Romanesque office building overlooks the grassy lot between Columbia and Marion streets east of Western Avenue, where the *Windward* still lies buried.

Further south along the waterfront, under Alaskan Way near the Washington Street Public Boat Landing, are the remains of Seattle's first hospital ship, the *Idaho*. An old sidewheel steamer built in 1860 for the Columbia River trade, the *Idaho* was tied at the foot of Jackson Street in 1900, and Dr. Alexander DeSoto opened the Wayside Mission and

Much tideflat filling had taken place by 1898.

tended south over the water on pilings to advance wharf building in that area. These street extensions and rail trestles served to define the outward boundaries for later landfill activity. As the network of trestles and street extensions grew denser, it became clear that it was merely a matter of time before the tideflats south of Yesler's Wharf would be completely reclaimed to create land for commercial and industrial development since the area was easy to fill.

A new shoreline along the waterfront north from Yesler's Wharf to Smith Cove, now Terminal 91, was also first staked out by railroad trestles. In Seattle's fervent desire to forge a transcontinental rail link, the city established a 120-foot railroad right of way over the waters of Elliott Bay, some 60 feet offshore. In 1885 the first trestle for the Seattle, Lake Shore, and Eastern line extended from King Street to Smith Cove.

As more railroad lines were added along the waterfront, the parallel series of railroad trestles, connected to the shore by timber walkways, became the beginning of Railroad Avenue, now called Alaskan Way. The area between the tracks and dry land was gradually filled using earth, wood wastes, ship ballast, and other refuse materials, and the shoreline grew westward, surrounding

Planked-over trestles and yawning gaps characterized parts of Railroad Avenue before 1936.

Seattle Engineering Department

Charity Hospital on board. The ship provided a haven of medical and spiritual comfort for the indigents of Skid Road. The year 1909 was her last year of operation; as the *Idaho* slowly deterioriated, she became part of Seattle's landfill and foundations. A plaque on the waterfront at the foot of Washington Street commemorates the *Idaho*'s service to the city.

In 1965 the old sternwheeler *Skagit Belle,* converted to a float-

g restaurant and night-
lub for the 1962 World's
'air, sank at her moor-
ngs at Pier 51. Problems

ad continually plagued
he vessel, and one morn-
ng the electric pumps
ailed, her bilges filled,
nd down she went. The
essel, with its pink and
vhite wheelhouse, re-
nained mired in the mud
or years, displaying
emnants of a slime-
overed sternwheel and
gangplank that dangled
om the pier. In March
973, the wreckage was
nally towed away.[1]

The steamer *Idaho* at the foot of
Washington Street.

the railroad trestles and eras-
ing the last vestiges of the
natural beach.

By 1890 industrial de-
velopers were eyeing the
tideflats in the lower reaches
of Elliott Bay. The city already
filled most of the available
level land, and steep bluffs to
the east and water to the west
limited further expansion.
Washington had joined the
Union in 1889, and when the
new state's legislature determined that publicly owned
tidelands could be sold to private individuals, the way was
opened for creating industrial
lands out of the flats. Beginning in 1895, extensive
dredging and filling in the
southern reaches of Elliott
Bay radically altered the
shoreline there. By 1905 the
East and West waterways
were completed and 300
acres of land had been filled,
including Harbor Island,
which was at that time the
largest man-made island in
the world.[6]

During this flurry of activity, the waterfront north of
Yesler's Wharf continued to
change on a piecemeal basis
until R. H. Thomson, Seattle's
city engineer, turned his attention to the problems that
he believed were frustrating
the city's growth: topography
and transportation. "Looking
at the local surroundings," he
later wrote, "I felt that Seattle
was in a pit, that to get any-
where we would be com-
pelled to climb out if we
could. I resolved to perse-
vere to the end."[7] While city
engineer, Thomson insti-
gated nine major regrades
and dredging and filling projects, including the Jackson
Street and Dearborn Street
regrades. One important
by-product of the Jackson
Street regrade was the use
of the waste material as fill
along the central water-
front. Four giant hoses
powered by electric pumps
spewed forth 6 to 10 million
gallons of water each day and
washed away the layers of
stratified blue clay and glacial
till. As a result, Jackson
Street's steep slopes were
lowered as much as ninety-
four feet in some places. The
sloughed material flowed
through wood-stave pipe at
an average of 4,000 cubic
yards per day to the open
spaces behind the rail trestles
and the still-soggy area
around Pioneer Square. The
Jackson Street and Dearborn
Street regrades created a
total of eighty-five acres of
land, and in some parts of
Pioneer Square the ground
level rose as much as forty-
three feet.[8]

Because these projects
raised street levels and not
buildings, what had formerly
been the street façade now
became a basement. The

result became part of Underground Seattle, and for some years pedestrians walked on trench-like sidewalks below street level. These were eventually planked over and buried, but reminders of this period in Seattle's history are still visible. Between University and Seneca streets just west of First Avenue is an exposed section of the old brick buildings that formerly lined the waterfront.

Thomson had even more grandiose plans for the waterfront, but they never came to fruition. In 1909 he proposed building a sea wall another one-half mile out into Elliott Bay to provide room for three new streets west of Railroad Avenue. Rather than curing a minor defect in topographic anatomy, this would have required radical surgery. It was estimated that the project would cost $17.5 million and require twenty years to complete. This idea soon faded into oblivion.[9]

Railroad trestles and landfills still defined the outer edge of Seattle's waterfront, but with these developments came the new problem of protecting the shoreline from eroding waters and hungry teredos, destructive woodborers capable of destroying an untreated piling in six months. Between 1911 and 1916, the city constructed a concrete sea wall from Washington Street to Madison Street, establishing the shoreline as it exists today on the southern portion of the central waterfront. North of Madison Street, Railroad Avenue continued to deteriorate as the rickety, wooden trestles began to collapse into the bay. As the situation worsened, some sections of Railroad Avenue had to be limited to light traffic and others were closed to any use at all.[10] In 1934 the city began to construct a sea wall from Madison Street to Pike Street, and by 1936 Railroad Avenue was finally converted from a wood-planked roadway to a filled and paved thoroughfare completely protected by a concrete sea wall.

The completion of the 1936 sea wall fixed the shape of the central Elliott Bay waterfront that exists today. Present-day visionaries, with proposals reminiscent of Thomson's plans to treat Seattle's topography like modeling clay, have directed landfill activity north and south of the central waterfront. Fill from the construction of Interstate 5 and gravel from a nearby island created the Myrtle Edwards and Elliott Bay parks on the northern waterfront. Some of the mammoth container terminals on the southern waterfront were formed by

A tideland rush of remarkable proportions began in 1888 — just before statehood. Seattle was bursting at the seams, and many people saw the level tideflats as the land of industrial opportunity, provided that this land could be filled.

Hordes of people tried all means imaginable — from cultivating oysters to building wharves far from the shore — to establish a foothold in the tideflats. Pilings everywhere marked parcels of property, varying in size from that of a city lot to forty acres. Disputes frequently arose, and as soon as one group made their so-called improvements, an opposing faction hired gangs to cut them down.[1]

Judge Thomas Burke' letter captures the mood

of the day:

Here in Seattle the craze for salt water has broken out again with greater virulence than ever before. A swarm of salt water lunatics, of high and low degree, have alighted, like so many cawing crows, on the mud flats in the southern part of town, and have made the place a veritable sight with piles stuck all over it. And herein is where there is a great abuse of charity by the sea—it should have drowned the whole of them, but so far, I am sorry to say, not a single man of them has even gotten wet.[2]

After statehood the battle slowed, but property values continued to climb, fulfilling one real estate promoter's earlier prophesy: "Get the tide-land habit; it will make money while you sleep."[3]

View of Harbor Island about 1925.

filling the spaces between the old finger piers. The Terminal 37/46 complex is one giant amalgamation of former Piers 37, 38, 39, 42, and 43 and Terminal 46.

The present-day shape of the waterfront represents one moment in a continuum of change. Although the most dramatic shoreline changes are now occurring in the south harbor and Smith Cove, proposals to expand the Washington State Ferries terminal would consolidate Piers 50 to 52. Other contemporary waterfront shapers have considered mooring large barges on Elliott Bay for expanded commercial and residential use. As it was in the past, the waterfront today is a dynamic place, subject to the changes in shape necessary to keep it a prosperous and lively hub of maritime activity.

Henry Yesler in the 1880s.
Photography Collection, U.W. Library

Map of Yesler's Wharf, early 1890s.

Birthplace of Commerce and Industry

The history of its [Yesler's Wharf] extension is the history of the growth of Seattle, every step of the one accompanying an onward step of the other.[1]

After brief stops in Ohio and Portland in search of the right place to establish a sawmill business, Henry Yesler arrived in Seattle in October 1852. Elliott Bay was perfect, but by that time all the good waterfront sites were already taken. Yesler prepared to resume his search, but instead he benefited from the pioneers' commitment to Seattle's growth. David Maynard and Carson S. Boren adjusted their own claims to give Yesler a prime waterfront location, and the townspeople immediately pitched in to help him build the steam sawmill that marked the beginning of the city's first industry. In those days, Yesler's sawmill sat on the beach at the marshy neck of the little peninsula where the Pioneer Place pergola stands today. The mill stood on pilings, which raised it above the water that washed under its western half at high tide. Other than a few houses and small fortifications, little else interrupted the forested shoreline of Elliott Bay.

Beginning with this sawmill, Yesler pioneered in most of the industries and business enterprises that eventually formed the mainstays of the economy of Seattle and the Puget Sound region. Known even in his own time as the "Father of Seattle," he was given to philosophizing with his friends as he whittled on one of the pieces of wood that invariably protruded from his back pocket. Although he was always full of entrepreneurial schemes and a vision of Seattle's great future, he never seemed able to pair his ideas with fully effective ways to accomplish them. Yesler would start an enterprise, but it required someone else to make it flourish, coupling Yesler's ideas with a little more capital and much better management. Nevertheless, he was successful in his own idiosyncratic way and died a rich man, even though many have said he prospered in spite of himself.

With the construction of a wharf in 1854 just west of his sawmill, Yesler began what became a "mania for wharf building."[2] Constructed of a few pilings planked over with rough boards, Seattle's first wharf was not a very sturdy structure. Over the years, Yesler dumped ship ballast and wood slabs at its base to help stabilize the shaky dock and to protect it from the wood-boring worms called teredos. Since this first dock extended just a short distance into Elliott Bay, ships could only land there at high tide, and often lumber had to be rafted out to the waiting vessels.

From these beginnings, Yesler launched a long, but lackluster, career in the Puget Sound lumber business. There were in all four Yesler sawmills. The first operated from 1852 to 1869, when Yesler completed the first major mill expansion. This second mill burned ten years later in 1879. In 1887 a third mill, built between 1881 and 1882, also burned. The fourth sawmill was built on Lake Washington and operated from 1888 to 1895 when it too was destroyed by fire.

Although the lumber industry fueled the early economic growth of the Puget Sound region, prosperity in milling passed Yesler by. In 1855 twenty steam mills operated

Ships loading lumber in the 1870s.

Puget Sound Maritime Historical Society, Williamson Collection

on Puget Sound. Some were processing from 50,000 to 70,000 board feet of lumber per day, yet Yesler's saws whined away at a rate of only 10,000. In spite of his renovations and expansions, Yesler never managed to make the mill more than marginally successful. He was continually plagued by lack of money, mediocre equipment, and lax credit practices. California's insatiable demand for lumber, along with a vast supply of good timber elsewhere in the region, served as the impetus for the development of numerous milltowns around Puget Sound, and other mills

Teredos!

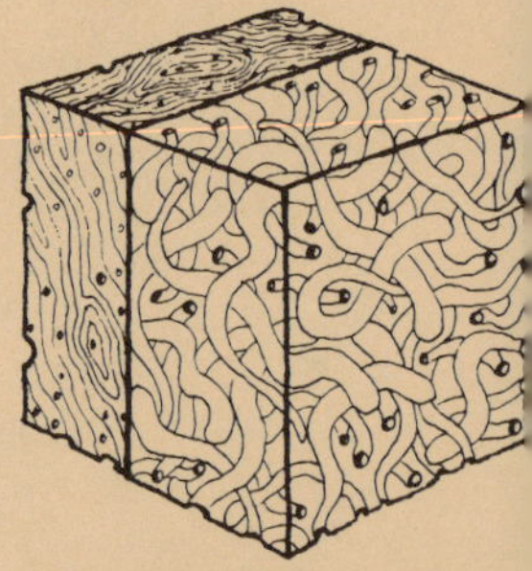

"The battle between man and the shipworm goes on, with the shipworm still getting somewhat the best of it."[1] Henry Yesler dumped tons of rock, ballast, wood slabs, and sawdust at the foot of his wharf pilings to stop these attackers. On June 16, 1877, the entire Pike Street coal bunker collapsed into the bay because of their incessant gnawing. The culprit was a shipworm with an unlimited appetite for wood, popularly known as the teredo (*Bankia setacea*).

The teredo is actually an unusual bivalve mollusk. It uses two small shells at the head of a long, worm-like body to rasp away at the wood, carving out neat, tubular burrows. Weaving a sinuous network around nails, bolts, and knots, teredos seldom break out through the piling's surface and rarely intersect a neighboring burrow.

It does not take long for shipworms to riddle a submerged wood piling until it finally gives way entirely. They can reduce an untreated piling to the point of collapse in six months, and even today a pressure-treated, creosote piling lasts only ten to fifteen years. Today most new pilings are constructed of steel-reinforced concrete to avoid the destructive worm.

achieved what Yesler's did not. Seattle soon faded in importance as a lumber town, but the Puget Sound timber industry blossomed and became the backbone of the state's economy until the turn of the century, when it was eclipsed by other industries.

By March 1859, Yesler had extended his wharf further into the bay. Two hundred feet long, it was still the only wharf in the small, waterfront community as well as one of the most spacious wharves in the region. It became the first wharf to serve the Mosquito Fleet, but in those days, passengers climbed slats nailed to pilings in order to get off the boat and onto the wharf, which stood high out of the water.[3]

Along with this extension, Yesler began to diversify his business enterprises. By adding a general store at the corner of Mill and Com-

"Commercial Row" at the foot of Yesler's Wharf in the early 1870s.

Early Mosquito Fleet steamers docked
at Yesler's Wharf.

mercial streets, now the intersection of Yesler Way and First Avenue South, and attaching a small patent grist mill to his sawmill in 1860, he could supply the day-to-day needs of the growing community. Yesler's Wharf was emerging as the nucleus of a major regional center.

Yesler's dabbling in flour milling anticipated the emergence of the grain industry as another important component of the region's economy. Grain grew well in the Puget Sound area, and the completion of the transcontinental railroad in 1893 opened the door to eastern Washington's breadbasket. In the first years of grinding flour, Yesler used the sawmill's steam plant to power the grist mill, but this was only a secondary business for him. He ran the grist mill at night when the sawmill was shut down, and this did not prove to be enough to provide flour for a growing city. By 1867 Yesler could produce twenty-four barrels of flour per day, but each of the twenty-one other grist mills located in the territory had a larger capacity.

Although he had originally planned to expand the flour business, Yesler's interest waned and he returned his full attention to lumber. Others in the area, however, pursued the grain industry. By 1875 the Stetson and Post grist mill had opened on Yesler's Wharf, and other mills soon located in the area as well. The growth of grain and flour exports that began with the completion of the transcontinental railroad increased in the 1920s with improvements in bulk-cargo handling. Grain and flour operations have since moved away from the central

waterfront but can still be found on Elliott Bay. Today large silos at the Fisher Mills on Harbor Island and at Terminal 86 are reminders of the early days when Henry Yesler first began grinding grain down by today's Pioneer Square.

Activity at Yesler's Wharf was a barometer of Seattle's increasing maritime commerce. Yesler made several small pier extensions in the late 1860s and early 1870s, but the next major one was between 1874 and 1875 to provide room for large coal bins serving the Renton and Talbot coal companies.

Transporting logs to the waterfront in 1880.

Yesler had already built a small coal bin on his wharf in 1864, but this new extension symbolized a commitment to the future of the region's coal industry. The addition formed a large wing jutting north from the end of the wharf, with the result that the whole structure resembled a large boot. Now extending 650 feet into Elliott Bay, the wharf could handle as many as six vessels simultaneously, loading lumber and coal as well as serving the growing steamer traffic.

In 1876 ten ships in port at the same time loading coal at the bunkers on Elliott Bay was an unusual sight, but the industry soon mushroomed, and five years later Seattle was described as the "Liverpool of the Pacific Coast."[4] By 1883 Seattle area mines were exporting 1.03 million tons of coal per year, much of it from Newcastle, east of Lake Washington between Bellevue and Renton. As had happened with his dabblings in the flour business, Yesler's involvement in mining declined as the industry grew. Other docks and coal bunkers on Elliott Bay continued to handle coal, which remained an important Seattle export until the 1920s, when the gasoline engine began to replace steam power.

By March 1877, Yesler's Wharf extended a full 900 feet into Elliott Bay, and in the 1880s more buildings were added. In 1882 Robert Moran, who later gained national fame as a ship-builder, set up a boiler shop on the wharf, and Yesler opened his third sawmill. Saloons were also a popular addition, sometimes called an important "lubricant" for Seattle's growth.

As Seattle's commerce increased, so did the hustle and bustle on Yesler's Wharf. By 1880 Seattle was the focal point of trade in the Puget Sound area, and Yesler's Wharf was the focal point of trade in Seattle. In 1882 an incredulous reporter for the *Daily Post Intelligencer* wrote:

Never within the recollection of the writer. . . has Yesler's Wharf been so taxed with business as during the past week or two. Yesterday, for instance, it was covered with miscellaneous merchandise as never before, eight warehouses being full and a great quantity being spread out over the dock be-

King Street coal bunkers south of Yesler's Wharf.

The Eliza Anderson Docks at Yesler's Wharf

In 1859 members of the state legislature took passage on the *Eliza Anderson* to investigate plans for a territorial university at Seattle. After all the stops on the trip north from Olympia, they knew that a whistle blast signaled that the boat was about to leave her berth. Upon hearing the whistle early one morning, they quickly roused themselves from their beds at a nearby Seattle hotel and headed to the steamer's boiler room, which they knew to be a good place to weather

sides. This merchandise, with a dozen trucks and drays, a half-dozen light wagons, an occasional carriage, and three or four hotel wagons, made it almost impassable for pedestrians; while the activity, the business, the people coming and going, is to be seen at no time on any other wharf. . . north of California, except the wharf of the O.R. & N. Co. at Portland.[5]

In spite of all this prosperous activity, Yesler did not keep the wharf in good condition. He was often criticized and sometimes sued for gaping holes in the dock. Less watchful individuals would periodically have a salt-water bath when they dropped through rotting boards. Even Yesler was once incapacitated for several days after losing his footing and hitting his back on a projecting plank.

Henry Yesler's presence still lingers on the waterfront today. Overlooking Pioneer Square is his tribute to Seattle, the Pioneer Building, which he built in 1889 after the fire that destroyed most of the city. At the corner of First Avenue and James Street, the flamboyant

Yesler's Wharf was the commercial hub of the developing city.

the rainy, cold January voyage. In the darkness of early morning, they arrived at Yesler's Wharf and gathered around the warm, glowing furnaces of the ship's boiler room. After waiting almost an hour, the men became impatient and asked when the boat left for Olympia. The fireman responded politely, ''This sawmill does not leave for Olympia.'' In the dark January morning, the legislators had inadvertently wandered into the boiler room of Henry Yesler's sawmill.[1]

Romanesque Revival ediface sits on the site that was Yesler's first Seattle home. The original mill site to the west of the Pioneer Building was sold to the city in 1890 to create Pioneer Place and resolve old street-alignment problems along what is now First Avenue.

A dilettante by nature, Henry Yesler was one of the most important proponents of Seattle's early development. With his wharf and sawmill as a base, he furthered the growth of the Puget Sound lumber, coal, and flour industries; fostered the expansion of marine commerce in the region; and supported the city's development as a marine transportation center. The era of early Seattle commerce ended when Yesler's Wharf was replaced by the Pacific Coast Company pier in 1901. By now Seattle was a major West Coast port and the entire waterfront was alive with maritime commerce. The hub of all this activity had shifted as well, from Yesler's Wharf to Colman Dock, the home of the busy Mosquito Fleet.

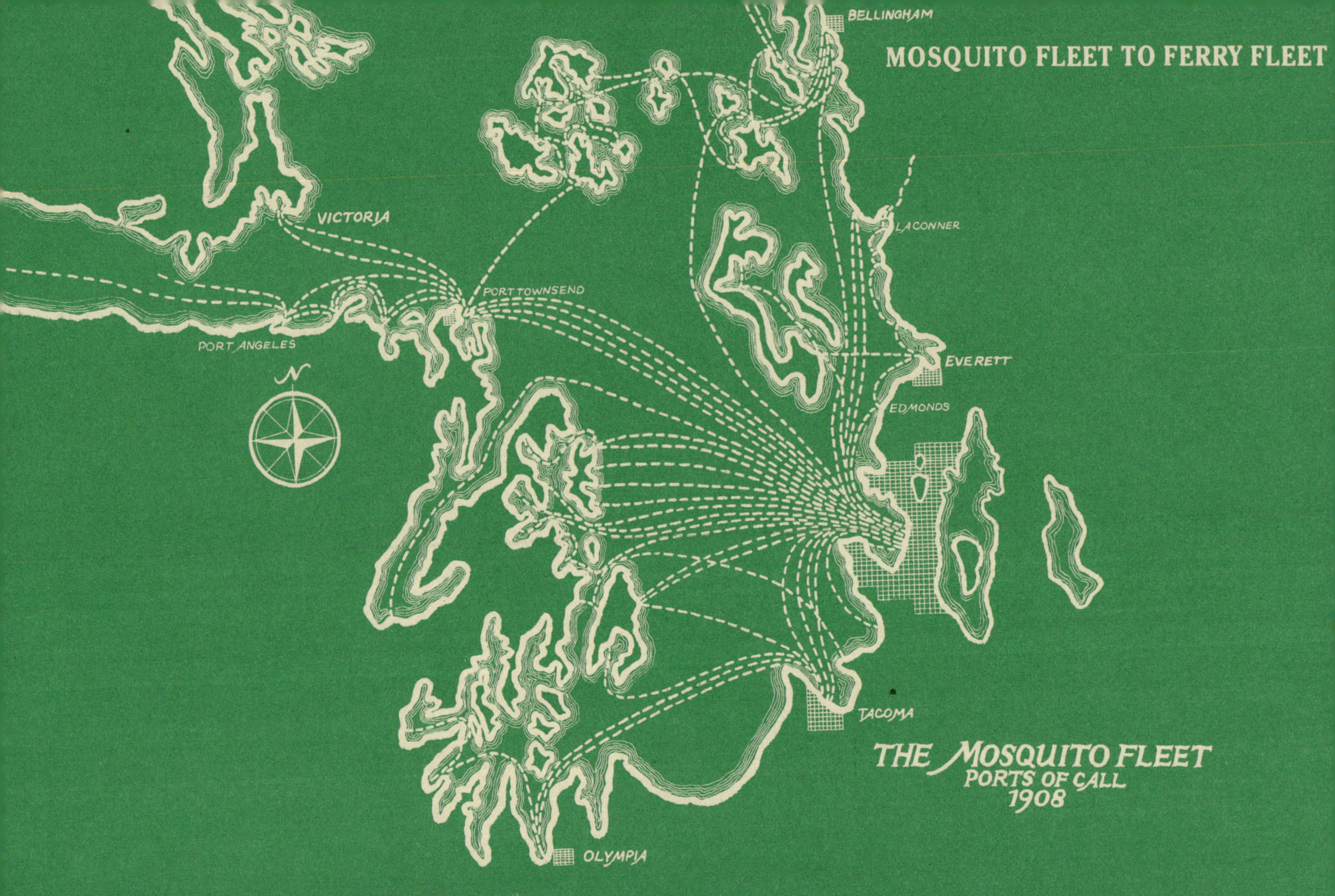

MOSQUITO FLEET TO FERRY FLEET
BELLINGHAM
LA CONNER
VICTORIA
PORT TOWNSEND
EVERETT
PORT ANGELES
EDMONDS
N
TACOMA
THE MOSQUITO FLEET
PORTS OF CALL
1908
OLYMPIA

Transportation Hub on Elliott Bay

In the days when there were no roads in the Puget Sound area, water provided the only link between settlements, and almost every community, no matter how small, had a dock or float. A collection of steamboats, known as the Mosquito Fleet, carried passengers, mail, and cargo on the inland waters of Puget Sound and in the San Juan Islands. This flotilla of small steamers was a conglomeration of individual enterprises, and in its heyday the bevy of boats with their white wakes is said to have resembled mosquitos on the surface of a millpond.[1]

Regular steamboat service to Seattle dates back to November 1853, when the *Fairy*, a sidewheel steamer built in San Francisco, began an Olympia-Seattle run. At that time, a connection with Olympia was vital since the only official U.S. Post Office in the Puget Sound area was located there. Less than a year later, the steamer *Major Tompkins* became the first vessel to operate an Olympia-Victoria mail route. Seattle was merely a way port on this route, which included stops at many other points along Puget Sound.

One of the best-known steamboats to come to Puget Sound in these years was the *Eliza Anderson*, a 140-foot sidewheeler brought here from Portland in 1859. Her name became a household word in the Puget Sound area during her forty-year career, and Yesler's Wharf was a regular stop on the Olympia-Victoria run that she made almost continuously for twelve of those forty years. During this time, she was a veritable gold mine for her owners, who in 1859 were charging rates of twenty dollars from Olympia to Victoria and fifteen from Seattle to Victoria.[2] These early years of prosperity provided the owners of the *Eliza Anderson* with enough of a financial cushion to enable them to rate cut when other boats began to compete for the mail run, and fares between Olympia and Victoria dropped to fifty cents. In succession the *Enterprise*, *Jenny Jones*, *Josie McNear*, *New World*, *Wilson G. Hunt*, *Alida*, and *Varuna* fought for the business, but the *Eliza Anderson* froze out the opposition.

When the Mosquito Fleet first began, passengers were picked up, sometimes even from row boats, and delivered to almost any point with little regard for schedules. On a single route, there could be more than a dozen stops. The Seattle-Poulsbo run around Bainbridge Island, for example, called at Scandia, Keyport, Brownsville, Venice, Enetai, Gibson, Westwood, Crystal Spring, Pleasant Beach, South Beach, Fort Ward, Seabold, Agate Point, and Port Madison. As one reporter observed in 1864, the boats were often annoyingly irregular, "Steamers come and go like a thief in the night and no man knows the day or hour."[3]

In the absence of roads, Seattle's central location within Puget Sound contributed to the city's emergence by the 1870s as a center of maritime activity in the area. All major communities along the water were situated within easy striking distance of Seattle by boat. Seattle's deep, protected harbor on Elliott Bay, which afforded a good, safe moorage, supported the city's development as the fleet's hub. By 1876 Seattle was home to more steamers than any other port on Puget Sound.[4]

Mosquito Fleet steamers berthed alongside Yesler's Wharf, about 1880.

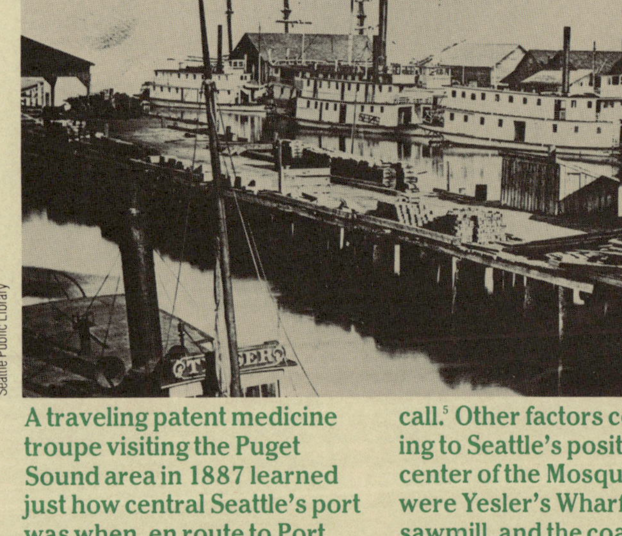

Seattle Public Library

Colman Dock during the Alaska-Yukon-Pacific Exposition, 1909.

The History of Colman Dock

A traveling patent medicine troupe visiting the Puget Sound area in 1887 learned just how central Seattle's port was when, en route to Port Blakely, Port Madison, Snohomish, Skagit, Port Ludlow, and the San Juan Islands, they had to travel back to Seattle after each stop in order to get to the next port of call.[5] Other factors contributing to Seattle's position as the center of the Mosquito Fleet were Yesler's Wharf, his sawmill, and the coal bunkers at the foot of Pike Street that had made Seattle an early trade and employment center. Ships came to Seattle from many world ports to load coal, sawn logs, and lumber.

By the 1890s, the Mosquito Fleet was entering a heyday that lasted until about 1920. Out of twenty-five steamer routes on Puget Sound at the turn of the century, nineteen stopped in Seattle.[6] Over the years, about 2,500 individual steamers were part of the Mosquito Fleet. Nearly all the boats were wooden until the early twentieth century, when steel-hulled boats began to take over the fleet. Originally, sidewheelers and stern-wheelers dominated, but later boats were propeller-driven, steam-screw vessels. The boats varied in length from 30 to 214 feet. On the average, they were 100 feet long and could each carry about 300 passengers.

Besides carrying passengers and mail, the fleet transported small cargo around Puget Sound. Farmers sent produce, eggs, and chickens

At the foot of Columbia and Marion streets, Pier 52 has been a nucleus of water transportation on Puget Sound since the 1880s. Colman Dock once stood at this site and was for many years the home of the Mosquito Fleet, just as the present-day terminal is the heart of Washington State Ferries.

The first dock was built in 1882 by James M. Colman,[1] a Scottish engineer who had come to the Puget Sound area many years earlier to operate a sawmill. Colman

was a respected mill-wright and successfully operated Yesler's Mill in the 1870s. Colman's first wharf was a light, 40-by-60-foot, wooden structure and rented for only twenty-five dollars a month.[2] In 1886 it was rebuilt and slightly enlarged but was destroyed during the fire of 1889. In 1890 a larger dock—100 by 192 feet—was constructed to serve Seattle's burgeoning trade and population.

In 1908 a much larger dock was built to centralize the Mosquito from the outlying farming communities to the Pike Place Market and Old Produce Row on the east side of Railroad Avenue, now called Alaskan Way. Leaving Seattle, the ships carried bales of hay, sacks of feed and oats, building materials, and food for grocery stores to the outposts. The atmosphere on the boats has been described by a former steamboat captain:

It was not long before it dawned on me that I was in love with this work. I liked these folk that rode our boat and never failed to have a pleasant "good morning" greeting, even though they wore nice clothes and perhaps had a lot of money. I appreciated the beaming smiles and friendly greetings of the farm ladies, too, who came aboard, especially at Poulsbo, Scandia, and Pearson on Saturday mornings

with their large heaping baskets of eggs. You see, as long as eggs were in baskets and carried aboard by themselves, they paid no freight, so on these mornings, the entire fore peak was filled with baskets.[7]

The Seattle-Tacoma run, a major route in the fleet's heyday, was one of the last to survive competition first from the electric, interurban streetcars and later—and more importantly—from the automobile. The *Flyer* started service between Seattle and Tacoma in 1891 and spent twenty-one years on the route. The slogan "Fly on the *Flyer*" was well known around Puget Sound and the boat's reputation was not undeserved. She set a record of one hour, twenty-five minutes, for the twenty-eight-mile trip between Seattle and Tacoma. By 1908 the *Flyer* had covered 1.3 million miles, a distance equal to fifty-one trips around the world, and had carried 3 million passengers.[8] In 1913 the 214-foot-long *Tacoma*, one of the largest and finest boats in the Mosquito Fleet, succeeded the *Flyer* on the run. The *Tacoma* was the fastest steamer ever to travel on Puget Sound and set a record of one hour, seventeen minutes, between Tacoma and Seattle.[9]

After World War I, the increasing use of automobiles stimulated construction of a road network that eroded dependence on the small steamers. The evolution to automobile-carrying ferries, beginning in 1916 with the *Vashon Island*, sealed the fate of passenger steamboats, although steamers continued to operate into the 1930s. Some of the old runs ended because the highway network was faster and cars were soon a cheaper and more convenient way to travel. Bridges eliminated the need for other runs, such as the Downtown-West Seattle run.

The most exotic of the new ferries was the *Kalakala*, the world's first streamlined ferry and a symbol of the end of the Mosquito Fleet era. The *Kalakala*, or *Flying Bird*, was the rebuilt San Francisco Bay ferry *Peralta*, which had been heavily damaged in a fire at her Oakland pier. At a Lake Washington shipyard, she was reincarnated as a 3,000-horsepower diesel ferry sheathed in a steel superstructure of silver-painted metal. Because of her unique appearance, the *Kalakala* was highly publicized, and thousands of people were on hand to watch her maiden voyage from Colman Dock in 1935. Some disapproving old-timers likened her appearance to a pregnant whale or a silver slug.[10]

The *Kalakala* was capable of an eighteen-knot speed, but she had an unfortunate tendency to vibrate. Her shakedown cruise was aptly termed—the vibrating shattered most of the upper deck windows and portlights. Before World War II, the *Kalakala* featured moonlight dance cruises. On the *Kalakala*, there was no need to move to dance, so vibrant was the cruise! After thirty-two years on Puget Sound, mostly on the Seattle-Bremerton run, the *Kalakala* was sold in 1967 and is now

Fleet, and at 705 by 110 feet it was the most imposing structure on the waterfront, considerably larger than its predecessors. A Romanesque clock tower on the outer end was 72 feet high and soon became a favorite harbor landmark. The dock's fourteen slips could be raised or lowered according to the tide.

This new dock remained in use until the night of April 25, 1912. That night, Captain John A. O'Brien was docking the *Alameda*, an Alaska Steamship Company liner, when a costly blunder occurred. The

ship's engineer accidentally set the engine at full-speed ahead instead of full-speed astern. The *Alameda* tore through the end of Colman Dock and smashed into the sternwheeler *Telegraph* on the other side, driving it into the adjacent Grand Trunk Pacific Dock, another dock servicing the Mosquito Fleet. The *Telegraph* sank in less than fifteen minutes, but no lives were lost, and the *Alameda* was almost unscathed.

The famous clock tower was found the next day floating in the harbor and was towed to West

Puget Sound Maritime Historical Society, Williamson Collection

The *Kalakala*, the world's first stream-lined ferry.

Puget Sound Maritime Historical Society, Williamson Collection

The sidewheeler *Eliza Anderson* at her Seattle dock.

Seattle. Shortly afterwards the outer end of Colman Dock was reconstructed, and a new more ornate clock tower was placed on the opposite side of the structure.

From 1916 on, automobiles were handled in increasing numbers. Around 1923 a short ferry slip to handle the bow-loading of cars was added, and in 1936 part of the old pier was torn down to make way for a terminal to better accommodate automobiles. The new Colman Ferry Terminal opened in 1937, featuring a fashionable, art deco façade. Eventually, this terminal proved inadequate to handle car and truck traffic because it had only a single-lane entryway.

Between 1964 and 1965, Colman Dock and the Grand Trunk Pacific Dock were demolished in order to make way

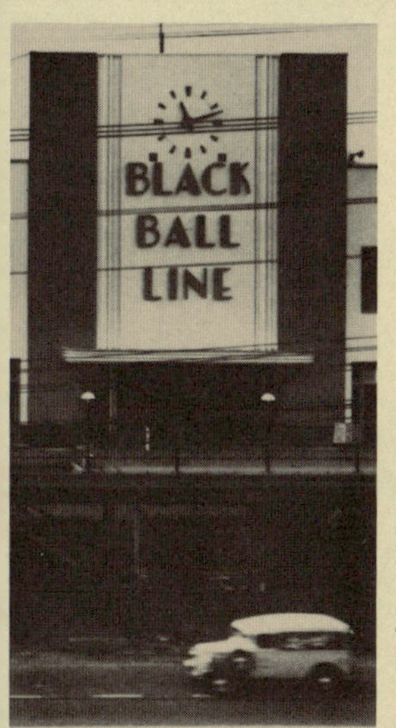

for the new Washington State Ferries terminal. Present-day renovation and expansion plans call for rebuilding the area from Pier 50 to Pier 52. Although the original Colman Ferry Terminal was completely torn down, its historic role lives on today because the site remains the center of the ferry system serving Seattle's busy waterfront.

Colman Ferry Terminal, 1937.

a crab-processing plant in Kodiak, Alaska.

As the modern era was being ushered in by boats like the *Kalakala*, the steamboat age was drawing to a close. One of the last freight and passenger vessels, the *Virginia V*, was taken off the Seattle-Vashon Island-Tacoma run in 1940. In 1973, as the sole survivor of the Mosquito Fleet, the *Virginia V* was placed on the National Register of Historic Places. Today she is still used as an excursion boat out of Seattle.

Following the Depression years, demands for automobile ferries increased, and those that existed operated at near capacity conditions. Over the years, the ferry routes were consolidated, as was ferry ownership, and eventually the Puget Sound Navigation Company, which had operated steamboats and automobile ferries

since its establishment by Joshua Green in 1903, had a monopoly on ferry service. In 1951, however, facing increasing costs and a drop in traffic, the Puget Sound Navigation Company sold the ferry system to the State of Washington.

Today Washington State Ferries operates one of the largest waterborne mass-transit systems in the world. As the hub of the state ferries, Seattle continues its historical role as the center of the Mosquito Fleet, with the major ferry terminal at Pier 52 on Elliott Bay. Nearly 7.5 million people used this terminal in 1980, about the same number as passed through Seattle-Tacoma International Airport. Although twenty years ago predictions said that cross-Sound bridges would spell their doom, the ferries are still an important means of transporting people

and goods on Puget Sound and in the San Juan Islands. A ferry ride today retains some of the magical appeal of the Mosquito Fleet days described by an old-time steamboat captain:

This "boat life" seemed to draw me; the smell of salt water, kelp and sea weeds were a tonic. The Puget Sound sunsets and sunrises do something to one's soul, whether he be young or old, that reaches beyond one's realm of imagination.[11]

GREAT NORTHERN
NORTHERN PACIFIC
YELLOWSTONE PARK
"See America First"
GREAT NORTHERN RAILWAY
GREAT
NORTHERN
RAILWAY
Burlington

Barricading the Waterfront

While many blame the Alaskan Way Viaduct for cutting Seattle off from its vital shoreline, it was the railroads that cut the waterfront adrift at the turn of the century when they fenced off the shore with their trestles. Bringing a railroad into Seattle was one of the pioneers' fondest dreams, and as this dream shaped the pioneers' actions, it reshaped waterfront development.

Although the region had a rich endowment of natural resources — coal, lumber, fish, and grain — these resources had little value without a market. With visions of creating a New York in the wilderness, Seattle's pioneers tried in 1872 to lure the Northern Pacific Railroad to select their city for its West Coast terminus. As bait the city offered no less than 7,500 town lots, 1,000 acres of land, $50,000 in cash, $200,000 in bonds, the use of the tidelands, and a depot location. In 1873, after much economic wheeling and dealing, the Northern Pacific instead chose Tacoma, at that time a small, isolated community in the upper reaches of Puget Sound.

Seattle's ambition could not be squelched for long. In May 1874, a festive picnic celebrated the first track laid for the new Seattle and Walla Walla Railroad, a company formed by Seattle citizens to build the city's own line across Snoqualmie Pass to the rich farmlands of eastern Washington. Despite good intentions, human energies and financing gave out; the completed railroad extended from the King Street coal bunkers only as far as the Newcastle coal mines near Renton, a grand total of fifteen miles. By 1880 the little Seattle and Walla Walla Railroad had gone bankrupt. It was sold and renamed the Columbia and Puget Sound Railroad.

The owner of this new railroad was Henry Villard, who had also taken control of the Northern Pacific. He offered to connect Seattle with his Tacoma terminus, and in their zeal to complete the transcontinental rail link, Seattleites willingly gave the waterfront to the railroad. In 1882, in exchange for Villard's completing this rail link to Tacoma, Seattle citizens presented him with a twenty-five-foot right of way along the waterfront. This right of way reached from King Street to Smith Cove, now Terminal 91, whose industrial potential was just being recognized. Not everyone gave Villard a right of way in the same place, however. Some waterfront owners wanted to keep their access on the street, while others wanted to retain land on the bay. As a result, the right of way was so convoluted that it earned the nickname, the "Ram's Horn Right of Way."[1]

Unfortunately for Seattle, Villard went bankrupt in 1884, and the Northern Pacific's new owners frustrated Seattle's growth by cutting the city's rail service. Once again, Seattleites responded by trying to bring their own rail line into the city. Because of the difficulties already presented by the Ram's Horn, the City Council created a mammoth new right of way. This one was 120 feet wide, located over the waters of Elliott Bay from King Street to Smith Cove beyond the line of high tide. This action, though illegal because the federal government still owned the territory's submerged lands, linked the futures of the waterfront and the railroads.

With the right of way established, little time was wasted in girding the shore with new rail trestles. The Seattle, Lake Shore, and Eastern Railroad incorporated in 1885 and took the inner thirty feet, building Seattle's first over-water trestle. In 1887 a 16,640-foot-long trestle built by the West Coast Railroad from downtown to Smith Cove became the second. On October 12, 1891, the Seattle and Montana Railroad completed its line from Seattle to New Westminster outside Vancouver, British Columbia, on a sixty-foot-wide right of way.

Seattle's dreams were finally realized in 1893, when the Great Northern Railroad selected Seattle for the terminus of its transcontinental line. The new railroad's right of way was also located in the growing conglomeration of trestles, later known as Rail-

July 4, 1893, was the long-awaited day. Seattle celebrated the arrival of James Hill's Great Northern Railroad, the city's first transcontinental line, with what was probably the grandest ceremony in Northwest history. Thousands of people poured into Seattle for the bicycle and torchlight parades, songfests, speeches, and dances.

Centerpiece for the festival was the "Coal, Lumber and Mineral

46

*Palace" on Pioneer
Square, an elaborate and
ingenious showplace for
the resources of the ter-
ritory. Over the north entrance of the palace was
a design in electric lights
symbolizing the union of
St. Paul and Seattle by
the locomotive, "J. J. Hill."
It was proudly described
as consisting of "about
500 electric lamps...
and the lights forming
the wheels of the locomo-
tive flashing in and out so
as to cause the illusion
that the engine is in
motion."[1]*

road Avenue. With the arrival of the Great Northern, the character of the waterfront began to change. No longer the hub of diverse city activity, the waterfront became the railroad's domain. For the next forty years, the tracks, continually filled to capacity with rail cars, formed a barricade between the waterfront and the heart of downtown.

By 1895 three transcontinental railroads—the Great Northern, the Northern Pacific, and the Union Pacific—owned most of the waterfront piers, and they all operated separate facilities. Competition among the various lines now began in earnest—tracks multiplied and the end result was chaos. Railroad Avenue was a series of planked-over trestles ribbed with parallel railroad tracks and had become "a confused jumble of switch-ings, crossings and backed up cars."[2] Trains ran at all hours of the day and night.

In January 1895, Virgil Bogue, a nationally known railroad engineer and author of the first major Seattle city plan, lambasted conditions on Railroad Avenue, describing the thoroughfare as unsightly and dangerous.[3] Only those with work or business there ventured to the waterfront. Pedestrians could cross the chaos only by using one of the overpasses located at Pier 66, Pike Street, and Colman Dock at Marion

By 1904 a maze of tracks and trains severed the waterfront from downtown.

Historical Society of Seattle and King County

Street, the site of the presen day ferry terminal. Because there were no warning signals, crossing the tracks on foot meant risking life and limb.

In addition to the confusic caused by the jumble of rail lines, there were separate passenger stations and depots for each railroad. Wher the Great Northern first came to town, it used a little wooden depot formerly operated by the Seattle, Lake Shore, and Eastern at the fo of Columbia Street on Western Avenue. Seattleites now wanted a grander depot, befitting their new status as an up-and-coming metropolis. In 1899 the Northern Pacific Railroad announced that it had purchased land along the waterfront between Washington and University streets to build a monumen tal depot and terminal. The $500,000 project was to

Railroad Avenue at the turn of the century.

cover four entire blocks of the central waterfront and include a new passenger depot and vast freightyards.

Although many applauded the idea for its boldness and grandeur, James Hill, President of the Great Northern, voiced the attitude that finally prevailed: "If you put such an obstruction across the front of your city, you will commit commercial suicide. You cannot obstruct traffic without driving traffic away. It would be a grave mistake for the city to make."[4] Instead he offered to build a tunnel under the heart of the city and put a depot where King Street Station stands today. Although the idea was dubbed "Hill's Folly" by some, the proposal was accepted.[5]

The tunnel project, a joint effort of the Great Northern and the Northern Pacific, began in May 1903. On January 2, 1905, the last crew walked out of the completed tunnel.[6] The two-track tunnel, which is still in use today, is 5,141 feet long and 30 feet wide. From its southern portal at Fourth Avenue and Washington Street, it runs under the heart of the city and exits near Virginia Street. Upon completion the tunnel was described by Seattleites as "the longest tunnel in the world—running from Washington to Virginia!"[7]

At that time, people thought the tunnel would alleviate railroad congestion along the waterfront. Although this was true at first, railroad squabbles continued and congestion on the whole grew worse. By 1909 the Chicago, Milwaukee, St. Paul and Pacific Railroad arrived

Silk Trains

in Seattle and became the fourth transcontinental railroad vying for space along the city's waterfront. Each railroad continued to maintain separate tracks, switching yards, and storage yards. There were 213.4 miles of tracks within the city limits,[8] and the duplication of switch engines and crews caused endless and unnecessary delays. Getting a railroad car from one end of the waterfront to the other could involve two or more switches and take as long as two days. This description of switching in 1914 typifies the waterfront headaches:

Many of the piers and docks along the entire waterfront are open only to switching… mainly by the Northern Pacific.… If, for instance, the Milwaukee [Railroad] wants to move a car from Pier 6 (Milwaukee Dock) to Pier 5 (Northern Pacific Dock), the Milwaukee must take it to the Stacy Street interchange yards, a mile south, notwithstanding the distance from Pier 6 to Pier 5 is only about 150 feet, and in due course of time, probably 24 hours, the Northern Pacific will set the car in to Pier 5, making the two miles round trip with a day's delay. This is an example of Seattle Terminal red tape for moving a car from one pier to an adjacent pier, with an extra charge for each switching movement.[9]

The lack of railroad-traffic police and city laws on railroad traffic made congestion worse. Crossings were unregulated and usually crowded with cars, and teamsters often left their wagons on the tracks all night, immobilizing traffic. Junk dealers dumped scrap on the tracks wherever they wished. The result was incredible traffic bottlenecks; the maximum speed in congested spots along the waterfront was a sluggish five miles per hour.

The formation of the Port of Seattle in 1911 was in part a direct response to the headaches and inefficiencies created by the railroads. The new Port Authority began to break the stranglehold that the railroads had on the waterfront by repurchasing a few of the piers to develop a public port. Before the end of the 1930s, the zenith of railroad power on the waterfront had passed. During World War I, the railroads served to support, rather than control, other expanding waterfront industries, such as shipbuilding and international trade.

A crowded Railroad Avenue still separated the waterfront from the rest of the city, but instead of trains, automobiles and trucks became the agents of congestion. Cars, in fact, squeezed

The opening of trade with the Orient in 1896 brought a host of exotic goods to the West Coast, the most luxurious of which was silk. By 1910 Seattle was the nation's hub of a burgeoning silk trade, and large ships, loaded with the precious cargo, docked in Smith Cove every three weeks. At the peak of the trade in the 1920s, raw silk accounted for almost one-half of the imports arriving in Seattle. In 1929, $151 million worth of silk passed through Seattle's port.

Historical Society of Seattle and King County

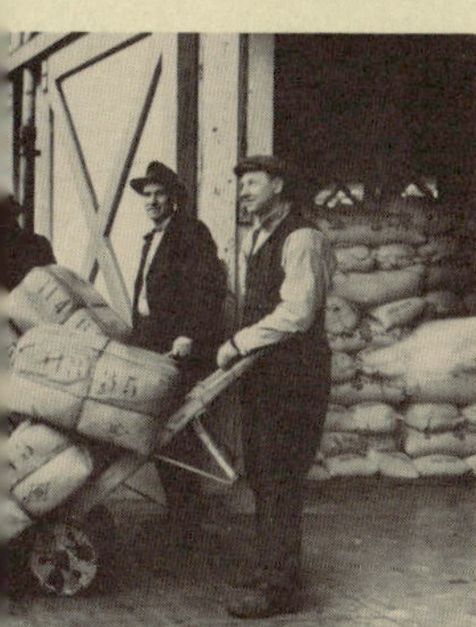

Seattle was an interim stop for the silk on the way to weaving mills on the East Coast. The raw-silk threads arrived in burlap-wrapped bales, each weighing about 132 pounds. Because these threads were perishable at extreme temperatures, it was often necessary to specially seal rail cars to protect the delicate fiber. Due to its fragility and the fluctuations in the price of raw silk because of heavy speculation, the silk was sped from Japan to New York. A special train, equipped with the

By the 1930s cars caused congestion near the ferry terminal.

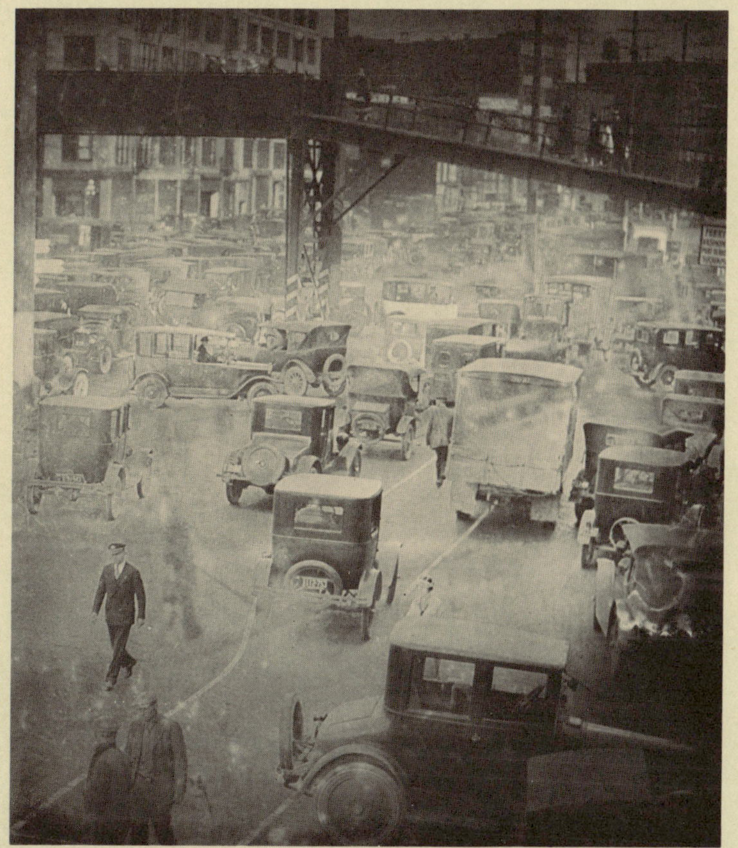

Puget Sound Maritime Historical Society, Williamson Collection

trains off Railroad Avenue through the tremendous increases in downtown automobile traffic in the 1930s. The ensuing auto congestion led to the construction of the Alaskan Way Viaduct so cars could skirt the clogged downtown core. First opened in 1953, the new viaduct epitomized Seattle's shift from the rail to the motor age since its construction eliminated several rail tracks.

With the consolidation and emergence of the Burlington Northern Railroad in 1970, it and the Union Pacific are the two major railroads operating in Seattle. Rail activity along the central waterfront has declined in recent years, and only a handful of trains use the old lines each day. Much of today's railroad activity, like other waterfront industries, has moved north and south of the central waterfront.

52

The location has shifted, but rail transportation is becoming competitive once again. The boom in containerized cargo shipping has been a boon for the railroads. Freight that once moved by ship through the Panama Canal is now unloaded in Seattle and transferred to rail cars for the remainder of the journey to East Coast destinations.

Although Alaskan Way no longer teems with trains, there are tangible reminders of the railroad's indelible influence on the shape of today's waterfront. Railroad tracks that once carried cars filled with cargo from the Orient and other world ports still lace the piers. Overpasses, like the one allowing pedestrians to safely cross to catch a ferry at Colman Dock, still exist at Marion Street and several other spots along the waterfront. The piers and transit sheds designed to handle the flow of cargo that moved between ships and trains retain much of their same form. Alaskan Way, the broad thoroughfare that once separated the waterfront from the rest of downtown, still girds the shore.

Causing endless headaches and congestion, the railroads effectively severed the waterfront from the rest of downtown Seattle, but at the same time, they forged an all-important link between water- and land-based trade and transportation. Without the railroads to speed raw materials, goods, and people to and from the interior of the Northwest and the East Coast, Seattle would have been stranded from both its resource suppliers and its markets. The coming of the railroads fostered Seattle's emergence as a leading maritime city.

fastest engines available and crack train crews, awaited the arrival of a silk ship at the dock. Immediately after the silk bales were loaded, the train set off for the East Coast. A fully loaded train carried as many as 5,000 bales of silk valued over $5.5 million. Armed guards accompanied every train.

These silk trains carried special white flags and took the right of way from any mail or passenger train in their East Coast dash. Stops were made only to pick up water or more coal for the steam engines and to change crews every 400 miles. Speed records toppled. The fastest trip

Photography Collection, U.W. Library

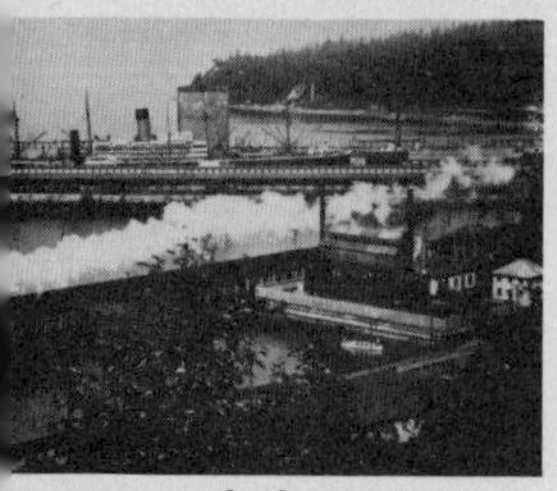

ever recorded was in August 1924. The ship *President McKinley* left Yokohama loaded with 2,286 bales of silk; the shipment was transferred to a train in Seattle and arrived in New York a total of twelve days, one hour, and fifteen minutes after leaving Japan.[1]

The first silk train left Seattle in 1909 and the last one sometime around 1933. As Japan began to export larger quantities of finished cloth from its own mills and as American-made rayon and then nylon gained popularity in this country, the silk trains became a thing of the past.[2]

Rail trestles at Spokane Street link downtown to West Seattle.

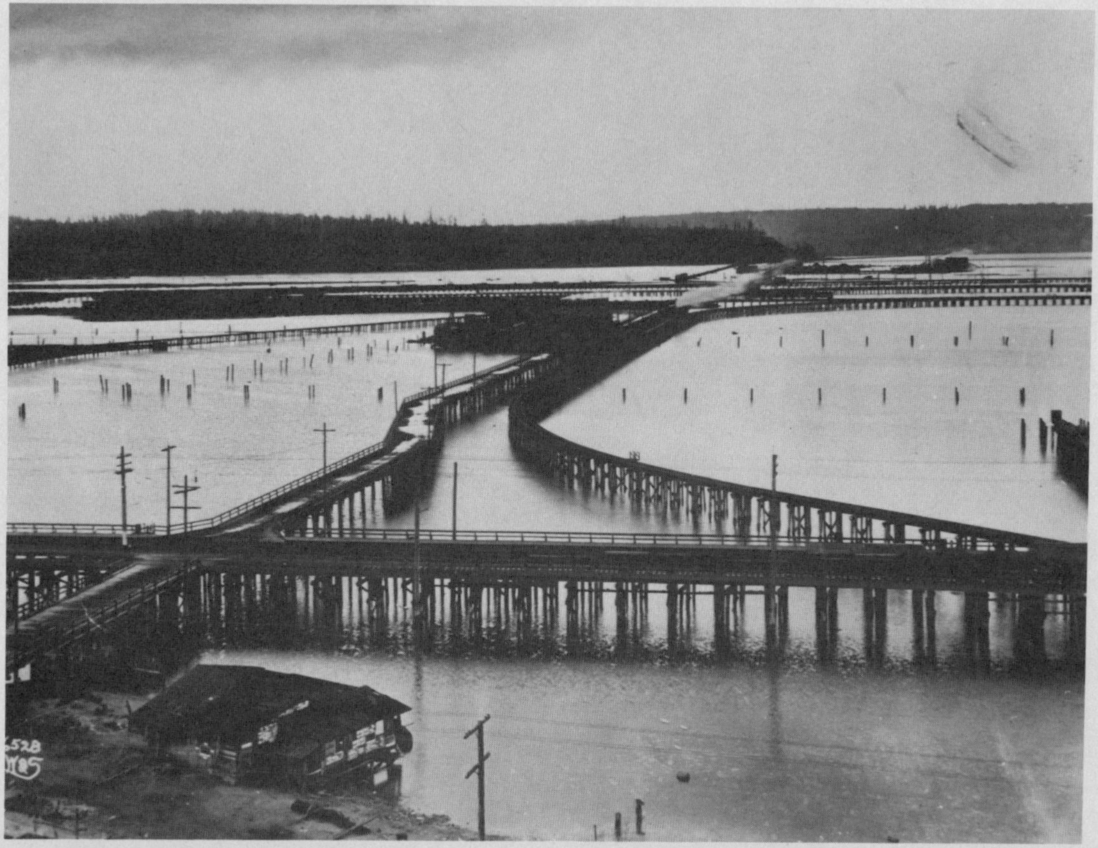

Historical Society of Seattle and King County

THE GOLD RUSH

SEATTLE BOOMS!

So far as Seattle is concerned, the period of depression which has lasted fully four years, is at an end. A period of prosperity, far greater than anything known in the past, is immediately at hand; has, indeed, already set in; and Seattle, during the next few months, will see the most wonderful growth and expansion of business which has ever been noted in any city on the American continent within the same period of time. This is not a roseate dream, or an enthusiastic prediction. It is the bold statement of a self-evident fact. [1]

In July 1897, only four days after the S.S. *Portland* arrived with a cargo of gold at Seattle's waterfront, this euphoric report accurately predicted the staggering effect the Gold Rush would have on Seattle.

In August 1896, eleven months before the *Portland*'s arrival, gold was discovered on the Klondike River in northwestern Canada. Some prospectors immediately headed to the Klondike to seek their fortune, but the gold fever epidemic began in earnest on July 17, 1897, when the *Portland* docked in Seattle. The excitement started to mount on July 15 when the *Excelsior* arrived in San Francisco with a cargo of gold. Once the word was out that an even richer treasure ship was due in Seattle, the *Post-Intelligencer* loaded a chartered tug with reporters to intercept the *Portland* as she entered Puget Sound. The newspaper's sensational edition hit town at about the same time the *Portland* docked and marked the beginning of a successful media campaign that enabled the city to capitalize on the benefits of the Gold Rush. That morning at six o'clock, somewhere between 2,000 and 5,000 people crowded onto Schwabacher's Wharf, present-day Waterfront Park, to meet the *Portland* which was reputed to be arriving with more than a ton of gold on board.

The truth was that there were more than two tons aboard the *Portland*. The ship carried sixty-eight miners, with approximately $700,000 in gold. No one had less than $7,000 worth, and several had $100,000 or more. [2] Crowds at Schwabacher's Wharf cheered when the miners hoisted their sacks full of gold. One man, named Nils Anderson, who had left penniless two years before, greeted his wife at the dock with three bags of gold worth $112,000. [3]

Seattle went berserk. By half-past nine that morning, downtown streets were so congested that some streetcars were unable to run. Passage to Alaska on the *Portland*'s return trip was booked almost immediately. Massive resignations started at once, including that of Seattle Mayor W. D. Wood, who wired his resignation from San Francisco and went off to join the prospectors. Within ten days of the *Portland*'s arrival, 1,500 people had left the city. [4]

There were almost as many entering Seattle as were leaving it, however, and many people in the business community stayed to reap the benefits of the prosperity which they expected would flow into Seattle during the Gold Rush. The docks were bustling. Streets were clogged with people, animals, and stacks of supplies. Hotels were full; people slept in the streets and stables

The wreck of the *Eliza Anderson,* near Dutch Harbor, Alaska in about 1898.

The Eliza Anderson's Last Voyage

56

and washed at fire hydrants. By the end of August, about 2,000 people had come to Seattle en route to the Yukon.[5]

Seattle was a logical point of departure for the Klondike, being 800 miles closer to Alaska than San Francisco, one of its chief competitors.

Portland, Tacoma, Victoria, and Vancouver, British Columbia, also competed for the Gold Rush trade, but the two most popular routes to the Klondike were both via ships leaving from Seattle. One was to St. Michael near the mouth of the Yukon River, where passengers traveled via riverboats to Dawson City, the major prospecting center. The other, shorter route was by ship to Dyea or Skagway and then over the White or Chilkoot passes to Lake Bennett and upriver to Dawson.

Along with Seattle's natural location as a departure point for the gold fields — a fact much used for publicity — the city also gained the lion's share of the Gold Rush trade because of a very carefully planned local advertising campaign. This was the era of sensational journalism, and Erastus Brainerd, secretary of the Chamber of Commerce Advertising Committee, was its spokesman. As part of Brainerd's effort to boost Seattle as the only possible outfitting port, the city's advertising in the nation's press exceeded other cities by at least five-fold. A special

Condemned and virtually worthless, the *Eliza Anderson* was abandoned at Dutch Harbor en route to the gold fields, and the passengers chartered another boat for St. Michael. By 1898 the wreck lay on the beach at Dutch Harbor. This note, discovered in an old whiskey bottle floating in Elliott Bay, tells one version of her story.[1]

August 30, 1897

Today I am sure our end is near so I will recount the tale of this disastrous voyage before it is too late. I sensed even before I boarded the Eliza Anderson that the ship

was doomed. In my frenzy to reach the gold fields, I booked passage on this 40-year-old vessel which has been resurrected to carry passengers to Alaska.

One of the first indications of trouble came when we found out that duplicate tickets had been sold—not an uncommon practice in these money-hungry days. Several men were so upset that they tried to hurl the ship's purser into the Sound before we left Seattle.

We left amidst much fanfare on August 10, as part of a flotilla of five vessels. Shortly after the

Klondike edition of the Seattle *Post-Intelligencer* was sent to postmasters, libraries, and mayors across the country. Brochures were distributed to the Great Northern and Northern Pacific railroads, aimed at reaching prospectors headed for the West Coast. Complimentary Christmas gifts, which included news of the Klondike, were sent to the crowned heads of Europe. Brainerd quoted the correspondent of *Harper's Weekly* on the superiority of Seattle as the place to set out for the Klondike, neglecting to mention that he himself was that local correspondent.[6]

Although Seattle was not initially prepared to handle the stampede of prospectors, every effort was made to locate and equip or build additional ships. Anything that could float was pressed into service. Ships that had long

The *Roanoke* brought $3 million in gold to Seattle, July 19, 1898.

been abandoned, even some that had sunk to the bottom of Puget Sound, were resurrected and hurriedly put on Alaska runs. Outbound ships were overloaded with people, supplies, horses, cattle, and other animals. Because large boats had not been needed before the Gold Rush, many ships used for Alaska service were small; sometimes five times as many passengers as a boat could safely accommodate were crammed on board. One ship was so overcrowded that, during a storm, the captain was forced to lock forty-four men in the hatches with the horses to lower the center of gravity. A burst of shipbuilding activity in Seattle was stimulated by the Gold Rush. In 1898 alone, Seattle shipyards built fifty-seven steamers, thirteen tugs, and seventeen steam barges and scows.[7]

By 1898 Seattle was the undisputed commercial and transportation gateway to Alaska and the Yukon, primarily because of the successful "selling of Seattle" as the port of departure for the Klondike and the efforts of the city's shipbuilders and merchants to handle the onslaught of prospectors. Seattle had garnered $25 million in Klondike trade by the spring of that year, compared with $5 million that went through other ports.[8]

The effects of the Gold Rush on the city were staggering. Merchants who had previously sold an annual total of $300,000 worth of goods received $10 million in outfitting in 1899 alone.[9] The timing of the Gold Rush coincided with the coming of the transcontinental railroad and the beginning of trade with Asia, and the city's population, as well as its economy, boomed. In 1899, 1,200 new homes were built in Seattle. The population jumped from about 43,000 in 1890, to 81,000 in 1900. The growth momentum continued beyond the initial impetus of the Gold Rush, and by 1910 Seattle's population had skyrocketed to 237,000.

The Gold Rush boom marked the turning point in Seattle's growth from a frontier town to the commercial center of the Northwest. It brought the city out of a four-year depression, engendered by the nationwide panic of 1893. The Mosquito Fleet had already helped to establish Seattle as the transportation center for Puget Sound, and the Gold Rush expanded the city's trade area, establishing Seattle as the Gateway to Alaska. The city was also in a competitive position for trade with the Orient relative to the rest of the West Coast, because of the growth that accompanied the Gold Rush.

The Gold Rush was a colorful, exciting time, and the prosperity that resulted changed the face of the waterfront. During 1900 and 1901, Gold Rush prosperity helped to finance rebuilding of the piers, as new docks were constructed to serve the city's burgeoning shipping needs. The Gold Rush provided a new direction for Seattle that endures today, by establishing the city as the jumping off point for passenger service and trade with Alaska. Reminders of the rousing Gold Rush days in Seattle live on at the Gold Rush Museum in Pioneer Square and at Waterfront Park, where a plaque commemorates the landing of the *Portland* in 1897.

voyage was under way, I discovered how poorly the boat was equipped. Imagine a boat which lacks a propeller, up-to-date boilers, refrigeration and is even missing a ship's compass! The coal bunkers, too, were completely inadequate.

After several mishaps on our way up the Inside Passage, five passengers disembarked at Kodiak. Now, during a raging storm on the way to Dutch Harbor, we have lost sight of the other ships escorting us and run out of coal. Rumors on board are rampant. Apparently, when the coal sacks were being filled on shore, some of the crew members hid half of them so they wouldn't have to load the full amount. In the wind and rain, we have torn apart the coal bunkers and ship's furniture in order to provide fuel to keep the boat running.

The arrival of the S.S. *Portland* at Schwabacher's Wharf on July 17, 1897.

Seattle, 1891.

Seattle, 1904.

The Sawtooth Look of Elliott Bay

After the success of Henry Yesler's first dock-building venture proved that wharves were essential accoutrements for Seattle's trade and commerce, other piers began to spring up along the shore of Elliott Bay. Consisting of wood pilings topped by a platform of rough-hewn planks, the first generation of wharves were flimsy at best. Built in assorted shapes and sizes, they usually extended straight out over the water from adjacent streets and were perpendicular to the shoreline. In those early days, if trade surpassed the pier's capacity, an extension would be added or a new wharf built. With time the idiosyncrasies of individual wharf builders and random additions gave the Elliott Bay shoreline an uneven, sawtooth appearance.

From time to time, dramatic changes occurred along the waterfront, as when the fire of 1889 consumed thirty city blocks, destroying the entire heart of Seattle, along with every wharf, mill, and coal bunker from Union to King streets.[1] The piers were rebuilt as haphazardly as before, but they had four times their previous capacity.

At the turn of the century, there was another massive rebuilding of the waterfront wharves. The shoreline that emerged had a pattern and order that had never existed before. Most piers now extended due east-west in a tidy, parallel progression from Washington Street north to University Street. Although over the years spaces between some piers have been filled and other piers have been replaced, the same alignment persists to this day.

The radical departure from the former ad hoc pier pattern puzzled people for years. What prompted the change? There have been as many hypotheses as there are piers. Some say shipping requirements were the impetus for the change. When the piers extended out over the water in a northeast-southwest direction, ships arriving from the north were forced to go around the corner coming into berth. With the east-west alignment, vessels entering the harbor could proceed along a straight course from Elliott Bay's entrance directly to dockside.

Others maintain it was a matter of water depth and tree size. Because the bottom drops off steeply away from shore, the Northwest's tall, straight trees are not long enough to serve as pilings at the ends of long piers. Building the piers at a forty-five-degree angle to shore rather than at a right angle made it possible to build wharves 150 to 200 feet longer.

To still others, the railroads were the determining factor. For convenient cargo handling, freight cars needed access to the docks. Trains could not negotiate a right-angle turn, and piers built at an oblique angle to the shore allowed rail cars to move on and off the wharves with ease.

The most far-fetched story claims they were realigned to conform with a dictate from Washington, D.C., declaring that all streets in America should run north-south and east-west. Apparently, Arthur Denny, while laying out Seattle's streets, ignored the dictate and ran the streets northwest-southeast, paralleling the shoreline. Forty years later, R. H. Thomson, the city engineer, decided at the very least the piers could conform to Washington's wishes and aligned them east-west.[2]

All these hypotheses contain a grain of truth, but the realignment was actually cemented by an underlying pattern established in the 1897 tidelands replat.[3] Prior to statehood, when all submerged lands were owned by the federal government, upland owners built their wharves any way they pleased. Technically, this was illegal, but no one was around to enforce the letter of the law. After statehood, the first tideland plat, adopted in 1895, allocated the underwater property following the random pier alignment that had evolved over time.

Only one year later, a minor plat adjustment south of Washington Street brought to light more serious flaws whose correction required the complete replatting of two miles of the central waterfront between Washington and Mercer streets. Like spokes on a wheel, property lines projecting directly offshore converged at one point, limiting wharf development and causing heated conflict between adjacent property owners.

With the same panache they displayed when regrading Seattle's hilly topography, R. H. Thomson and the City Engineering Department decided to use this opportunity to solve the host of problems caused by the planless pier alignment. They devised a comprehensive new scheme which laid out all the lots on a parallel due east-west plan. Subsequent pier building would have to conform to this alignment.

The replat was officially adopted by the State Legislature in 1897. Despite the logic behind the action, most property owners at first resisted the change. George Cotterill, then serving as the state's agent for the readjustment and later elected Seattle mayor in 1912, spent two years trying to straighten out the submerged real estate tangles. In time, the Northern Pacific Railroad and the Pacific Coast Company, the largest property owners on the waterfront, were persuaded to readjust their extensive holdings. Their coffers brimming with profits from the Gold Rush and Orient trade, the two companies rebuilt their piers on a grand scale. Between 1900 and 1901, they spent a total of $2 million constructing seven spacious docks and warehouses. No longer a maze of lines on paper, the replat became an accomplished fact guiding the pattern of pier development that still persists today.

The Seattle Fire

The glue pot that started the Great Fire of 1889.

Midafternoon on June 6, 1889, a pot of hot glue boiled over in a basement cabinetmaker's shop at the corner of Front Street, now First Avenue, and Madison Street, starting the worst fire in Seattle's history. The fire spread rapidly, torching everything in its path including most of the waterfront wharves. Under the leadership of Mayor Robert Moran, the townspeople made valiant efforts to stop the fire, but with little success. Henry Yesler's fine

residence did survive,
however, saved by a
cover of wet blankets.
By the time the fire was
contained early the
following morning, the
entire heart of down-
town Seattle was in
ruins. Damage was esti-
mated at $10 million. For
a thriving young city like
Seattle, the fire was not a
death blow but a spur to
new growth. Businesses
immediately re-opened
on the same spot in
hastily set up tents.
Within a few years,
Seattle was entirely re-
built in enduring brick
and stone.[1]

Around 1900, the piers were rebuilt on
a parallel east-west alignment, at an
angle to the streets, shown here in a
recent photo.

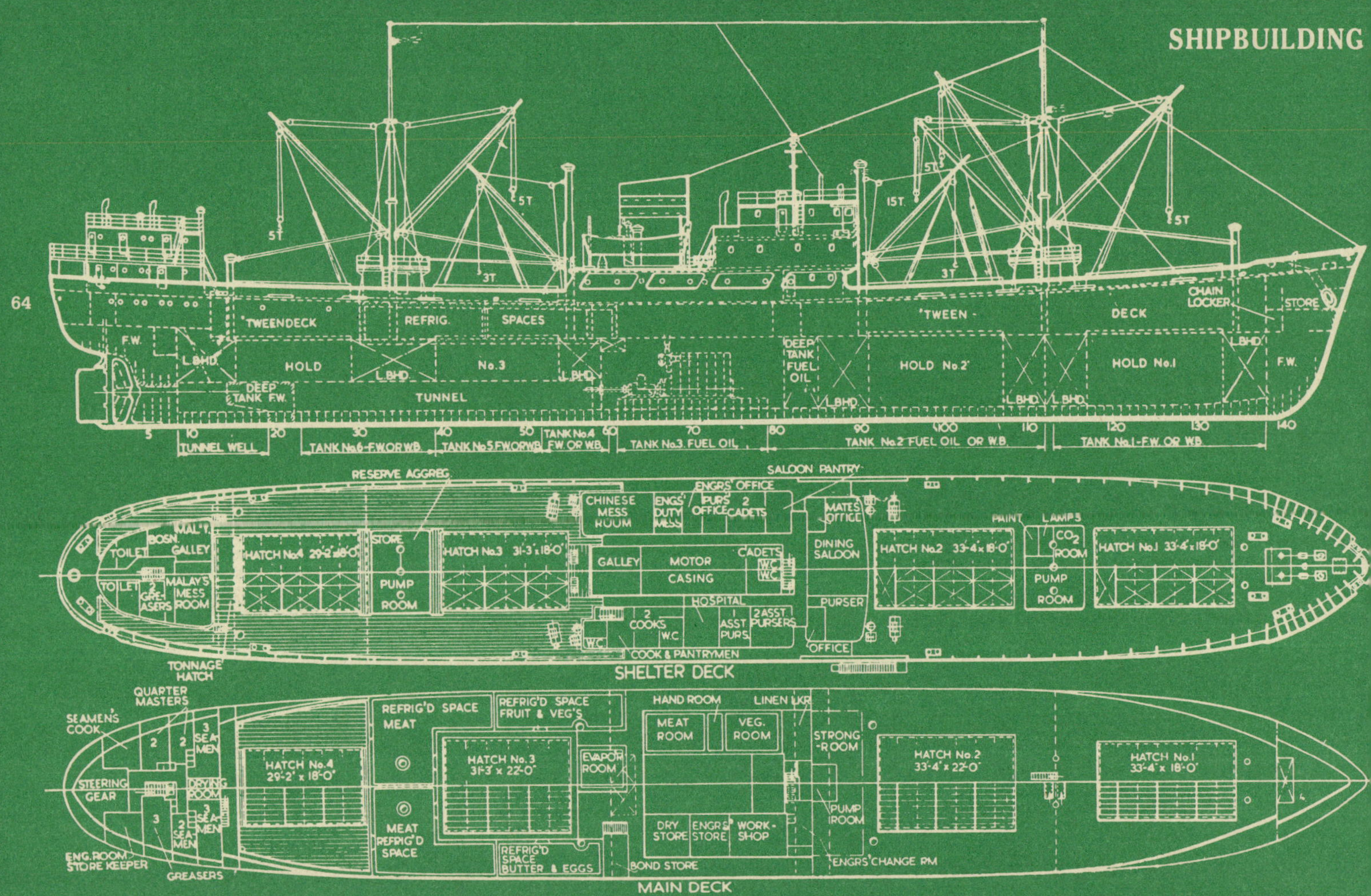

SHIPBUILDING
64
TWEENDECK   REFRIG.   SPACES
'TWEEN -   DECK
CHAIN LOCKER
STORE
F.W.
L.BHD.
HOLD   No.3
DEEP TANK FUEL OIL
HOLD No.2
HOLD No.1
L.BHD
F.W.
DEEP TANK F.W.
TUNNEL
L.BHD
L.BHD
L.BHD
L.BHD
L.BHD
5T
5T
3T
15T
3T
5T
5
10
20
30
40
50
60
70
80
90
100
110
120
130
140
TUNNEL WELL
TANK No.6 F.W. OR W.B.
TANK No.5 F.W. OR W.B.
TANK No.4 F.W. OR W.B.
TANK No.3 FUEL OIL
TANK No.2 FUEL OIL OR W.B.
TANK No.1 F.W. OR W.B.

RESERVE AGGREG.
SALOON PANTRY
ENGRS' OFFICE
CHINESE MESS ROOM
ENGS' DUTY MESS
PURS' OFFICE
2 CADETS
MATES OFFICE
PAINT
LAMPS
MAL'Y. GALLEY
BOSN
TOILET
TOILET
2 GREASERS
MALAY'S MESS ROOM
STORE
HATCH No.4 29'-2" x 18'-0"
HATCH No.3 31'-3" x 18'-0"
PUMP ROOM
GALLEY
MOTOR CASING
CADETS
W.C
W.C
DINING SALOON
HATCH No.2 33'-4" x 18'-0"
CO2 ROOM
PUMP ROOM
HATCH No.1 33'-4" x 18'-0"
HOSPITAL
PURSER
2 COOKS
W.C
1 ASST PURS
2 ASST PURSERS
W.C
COOK & PANTRYMEN
OFFICE
TONNAGE HATCH
SHELTER DECK

QUARTER MASTERS
HAND ROOM
LINEN LKR
SEAMEN'S COOK
REFRIG'D SPACE MEAT
REFRIG'D SPACE FRUIT & VEG'S
MEAT ROOM
VEG. ROOM
STRONG-ROOM
3 SEAMEN
2
2
EVAPOR ROOM
HATCH No.4 29'-2" x 18'-0"
HATCH No.3 31'-3" x 22'-0"
HATCH No.2 33'-4" x 22'-0"
HATCH No.1 33'-4" x 18'-0"
STEERING GEAR
DRYING ROOM
2 SEAMEN
3
MEAT REFRIG'D SPACE
DRY STORE
ENGRS' STORE
WORK-SHOP
PUMP ROOM
REFRIG'D SPACE BUTTER & EGGS
BOND STORE
ENGRS' CHANGE RM
ENG. ROOM STORE KEEPER
GREASERS
MAIN DECK

The Ups and Downs of a Major Waterfront Industry

In 1864 the construction of the *Black Diamond*, a seventy-foot, flat-bottomed steamer, started Seattle's shipbuilding industry, an industry characterized by great bursts of activity and great periods of doldrums. There were only a few boats built on Puget Sound before 1870, and this new Seattle enterprise grew slowly at first. Building and outfitting steamships for the Mosquito Fleet soon led to the production of ships for the ocean-going trade to Alaska and California. Other Puget Sound communities, such as Port Blakely and Port Ludlow, were initially the major shipbuilding centers of the region, but Seattle established a fledgling industry during the 1870s and used it as a springboard to developing a mainstay industry of the city's waterfront scene. From the first days when little wooden steamers were built on Elliott Bay beaches to 1895 at the end of the first three decades of Seattle's shipbuilding, seventy-six steamers, seventeen schooners, one barkentine, and nine tugs had emerged from Elliott Bay shipyards.

Typical of the boats built during this early era was the sidewheel steamer, the *George E. Starr,* launched August 12, 1879. The vessel was built by J. F. T. Mitchell at his yard on the beach between Bell and Blanchard streets, east of today's Pier 66. In those days, a yard consisted of little more than a woodworking shop and a patch of level ground on which to construct the boat. The 154-foot steamer was built for the Starr line, whose boats monopolized early Puget Sound steamboat routes. During her long and lustrous career, the classic-lined ship was considered the "crack liner of the Sound."[1] Her speed even enabled her to dog the heels of the aging *Eliza Anderson* and, at the last minute, steam ahead to the dock and snatch up waiting passengers.[2] Speed does not necessarily equate with stability, however, and the *George E. Starr* was also famous for carrying more seasick passengers than any other boat on the Sound.[3] As did many other boats, she abandoned her Puget Sound run in 1897 for the more profitable Seattle-Skagway route during the Klondike Gold Rush. Later she returned to Puget Sound and was finally dismantled in 1911.

The Gold Rush was a shot in the arm for many Seattle businesses, and it fueled the shipbuilding industry's first major growth spurt as well. Between January and July 1898, Elliott Bay shipyards launched a total of seventy-four ships. A leading figure in this growth was a man named Robert Moran, who had arrived at Yesler's Wharf from New York in November 1875.

Coming from a long line of ironworkers and shipbuilders, he first set to work in the machine and engineering trades. With a savings of $1,500, in 1882 he opened a small marine repair shop on Yesler's Wharf, then the focal point of Seattle's commerce and industry. He lost everything in the fire that destroyed most of Seattle's waterfront in 1889 but, undaunted, decided to consider this an opportunity to expand. Joined by his brothers and newly organized as the Moran Brothers Company, he selected a spot on the tidelands at the foot of Charles Street, near the site of what is now the Terminal 37/46 complex, to open their marine repair shop and shipyard.

There they had the room to expand that Yesler's Wharf and other central waterfront locations lacked, and the scale of their work soon increased dramatically. From boilers, engines, and pumps, the Morans branched into building complete ships, starting with the fireboat *Snoqualmie.* In January 1898, riding on the crest of the shipbuilding boom stimulated by the Klondike Gold Rush, the Morans began construction of twelve identical sternwheel steamers for the rapidly expanding Yukon River trade in Alaska. At the completion of the eight-month project, the dozen 175-foot vessels steamed en masse to St. Michael at the mouth of the Yukon River with Robert Moran as commander. Lloyd's of London insured the fleet for approximately $500,000, and only

one boat was lost on the trip across the treacherous Gulf of Alaska. Today the original log book of the voyage can be seen at the Klondike Gold Rush National Historical Park Museum across from Occidental Square.

Still heady from the Gold Rush boom, Robert Moran confidently submitted a bid to the Secretary of the Navy to build the battleship *Nebraska*, despite the fact that the Moran yard was a novice at building steel-hulled vessels. Although Moran had the lowest bid—in spite of stiff competition from long-established East Coast shipbuilders—it was still $182,000 more than the available appropriation. Seattle, however, was quick to support one of its favorite sons, and the Chamber of Commerce pledged $100,000 to help cover the difference. The Moran yard got the contract,

and the keel was laid July 4, 1902. Robert Moran personally supervised the project from the beginning until the 435-foot battleship slid down the ways October 7, 1904, amidst great fanfare and crowds "so thick one could have walked across the yard on their heads."[4] At the time, no other battleship surpassed the *Nebraska* in power or efficiency, and she was

later eulogized as among the best ships in the American Navy.[5]

The period of quiescence that followed the *Nebraska*'s construction ended in 1915. Events were fast catapulting the United States into a world war, and ships of all kinds were desperately needed. Fueled by federal contracts and capitalizing upon a strategic Pacific Coast location,

The *George E. Starr* after launching on
August 12, 1879.

excellent harbor facilities, and past shipbuilding experience, the Seattle shipbuilding industry began to boom. The central waterfront was too small to meet industrial needs, and most new shipyards followed the Morans' lead and located in the new industrial area created by filling the Duwamish tideflats. During World War I, Seattle shipyards set the pace for the rest of the country. No less than twenty percent of all the ship tonnage built in the United States for the war was constructed in Seattle.

When this phenomenal boom began in 1915, Seattle Construction and Drydock Company, who had bought out Moran in 1906, employed only 200 people and was the only yard building steel-hulled vessels. Less than one year later, 6,000 people were employed in several different shipyards, with the number

continuing to grow as new yards opened. In addition to Seattle Construction and Dry Dock, Skinner and Eddy, J. F. Duthie Corporation, and Ames Shipbuilding and Dry Dock Company established themselves that year, all soon becoming household names. By 1918 twenty shipyards — seven building steel vessels and thirteen building wooden ships[6] — were operating on the Elliott Bay waterfront, turning out submarines, destroyers, and both wooden and steel merchant vessels. An estimated 40,000 people were employed in the shipyards at the industry's peak in 1918.[7] Former farm hands worked side by side with lawyers and other professionals who, enticed by high wages, had left their jobs to don overalls in the shipyards.

The end of World War I was cause for celebration, but it also spelled temporary doom for the shipbuilding industry. Construction stopped on some unfinished vessels while other, newly completed boats never saw service. "Wilson's Wood Row" became a symbol of the industry's somnolence — some thirty completed wooden ships were moored on Lake Union when the war ended and remained there for many years before they were finally burned.

These signs of the shipbuilding industry's dependence on military spending were reinforced by the fact that many shipyards were forced to close after World War I. Shipyard shutdowns led to labor strife and strikes. Even congressional intervention, designed to pump up the industry, failed; the yards closed. Both the yards and the people who worked in them sat idle.

One shipyard, however,

filled a new need during the Great Depression. On an October night in 1931, eleven homeless men squatted in the empty Skinner and Eddy yard, starting the shanty town of Hooverville. Despite police raids and burnings, it grew to the size of a small city and had its own government. There Hooverville remained until the beginning of World War II, when the site once again became a shipyard building destroyers for Uncle Sam.

With World War II, the country was again scrambling for ships. As in the days of the Gold Rush, anything that could float was called into service. The veteran ships of World War I that had been languishing at their moorings were slow and inefficient, but they were suddenly in great demand. Almost overnight twenty-nine shipyards were operating in Seattle,[8] but none

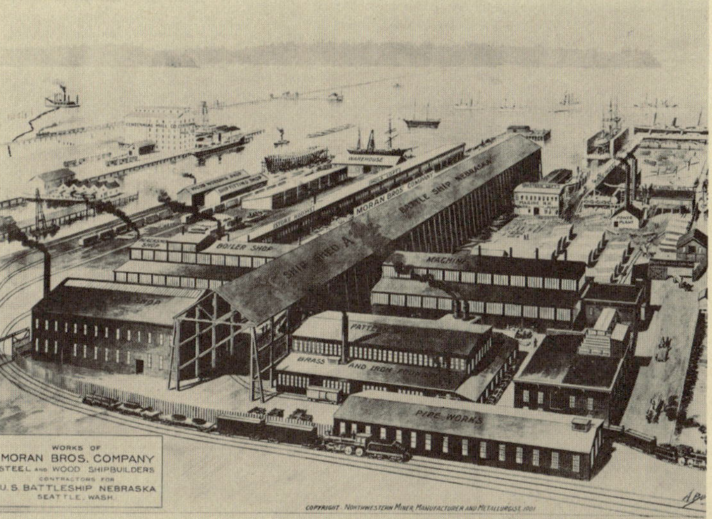

Historical Society of Seattle and King County

were located on the crowded central waterfront.

With welded-steel construction, the quantity and tonnage produced in World War II far surpassed that of the previous war. The Todd yard, who had purchased the old Seattle Construction and Dry Dock Company in 1916,

built forty-five destroyers and three tenders for the U.S. Navy between December 7, 1941, and August 31, 1945, at their yard on Harbor Island, an average of one completed vessel every month. During that time, they employed up to 7,000 workers at once.[9] Although they got their start

Hooverville, home of Seattle's unemployed during the Great Depression.

Photography Collection, U.W. Library

away from the central waterfront, Puget Sound Bridge and Dredging emerged as one of the most productive yards during the war. They produced forty-one minesweepers, four seaplane tenders, and numerous support vessels. At one point, they were delivering one completed ship every ten days. Other steel-fabricating yards produced escort aircraft carriers, landing craft, patrol boats, troop ships, tugs, barges, floating dry docks, and more,[10] while yards specializing in wooden vessels began to build a variety of auxiliary military craft.

Shipbuilding in Seattle again declined after World War II, but since the beginning of the 1970s it has boomed. Today it is Seattle's second-largest industrial employer, with 5,000 people working in the Todd and Lockheed yards alone. Todd Pacific Shipyards, descended from the Moran Company, and Lockheed Shipbuilding, who acquired Puget Sound Bridge and Dredging, are busy repairing and converting ships, as well as striking out in new territory in the development of modern, sophisticated naval vessels. Emerging from the yards are destroyers, destroyer escorts, ocean-going research vessels, submarine tenders, and guided-missile frigates, and Lockheed is currently developing new amphibious landing ships. In the early 1970s, Todd completed the *Spokane* and the *Walla Walla*, the "Queens of the Fleet," for the Washington State Ferries, and these both now operate on the Seattle-

The Speed Demons of World War I

The Seattle firm of Skinner and Eddy broke all national shipbuilding records in its day. On February 3, 1916, the owners stood at the site of their future yard, south of Seattle Construction and Dry Dock, part of today's Terminal 37/46 complex. The site was bare except for the remains of the old Sunset Engine Shop and a foot of snow. By October 21, 1916, less than nine months later, two 8,800 ton steamships, the *Niel Nielsen* and the *Hanna Nielsen* had been launched, while another keel was laid beside five

other ships in various stages of construction.[1]

Skinner and Eddy paced the country's World War I shipbuilding efforts, toppling world records along the way. Ships that required ten to twelve months to construct before World War I, Skinner and Eddy built in fifty-five days. In December 1918, they launched the *West Mahomet* in only forty-six working days.[2] During World War I, these speed demons completed and delivered a total of seventy-five ships, a full ten percent of all the steel vessels built in the United States in those years.

Winslow run. Unlike the early Mosquito Fleet steamers that could carry only several hundred passengers, these 440-foot ships can each accommodate 206 cars and 2,000 passengers.

Seattle has always possessed the necessary ingredients to support a thriving shipbuilding industry: a sheltered, deepwater harbor; available materials; and a ready pool of workers. In and around Elliott Bay today, shipbuilders are still actively pursuing their trade. Near the mouth of the Duwamish River, the Todd shipyard and Lockheed Corporation are producing some of the world's most sophisticated vessels. The Ballard yards make a variety of modern fishing boats, while other yards and dry docks on Lake Union and Lake Washington are kept busy with commercial ship repair and manufacture of a host of smaller vessels, such as the racing shells that often skim across Seattle's waterways. Although a permanent fixture on Seattle's waterfront scene, shipbuilding has always been an inherently fickle industry, intimately tied to changes in the national economy and political climate. Sensitive to changing industrial needs, the city has weathered the fluctuations by moving into the construction of larger and different types of ships and expanding operations to more spacious surroundings. As long as there continues to be a demand for ships, they will be built on Elliott Bay.

71

Port of Seat

Of Hand Trucks, Fork Lifts, and Containers

First men and then machines have moved the great assortment of cargoes that have crossed Seattle's docks. Like most other cities on Puget Sound, Seattle began its commercial career by exporting sawn logs, lumber, and later coal, to resource-hungry California in exchange for frontier staples — axes, boots, tobacco, coffee, and whiskey. The growth of the Mosquito Fleet, the opening of the Orient trade in 1896, and the Alaska Gold Rush in 1897 all helped Seattle to become a major trade center. Over the years, the early cargoes have been succeeded by a vast array of products. Exports have included apples destined for Saudi Arabia, pears for New Zealand, salmon for Europe, logs and cherries for Japan, and wheat for Russia. Into Seattle have come silk and tea from the Orient, rubber from India, cheese from Switzerland, coffee from South America, cars and oranges from Japan, and assorted manufactured goods from around the world.

Although the cargoes have become more sophisticated, for many years the methods of handling them did not, and up until the 1940s, longshoremen wielding hooks handled the ebb and flow of commerce across Seattle's wharves. In fact, their work methods had changed very little since the days of ancient Greece. Like their counterparts in Phoenicia who bore the wares of Egypt and Babylonia on their backs, sweating stevedores on Elliott Bay docks used only brute strength to help them move the inexhaustible supply of freight, piece by piece. Numerous gangs of men were continually employed in the slow and laborious process.

Break-bulk cargo, the name given to boxes and other goods — including whole frozen reindeer carcasses — moved item by item, was hoisted out of the ship's hold and landed on the pier. With brawn and hand trucks, longshoremen moved the goods into the transit sheds, or warehouses, where draymen retrieved them. Other, bulkier goods required even more strenuous loading techniques since they were moved in the aggregate. Coal, for example, was moved by bucket in and out of the ship's hold. Logs had to be hoisted or skidded aboard ship and then lashed to the deck.

The shape of early waterfronts, including Seattle's piers and docks, was largely dictated by this tedious method of moving cargo. The finger piers, so characteristic of Seattle's shoreline, are artifacts of the break-bulk cargo days, when long piers and boat slips were necessary so that a ship could unload its forward and after holds simultaneously. These narrow, parallel slips and piers also allowed more efficient use of limited waterfront space. Each pier had a long, narrow apron, or open area where cargo was landed, and a large transit shed, where the longshoremen stored the freight to protect it from inclement weather before reloading it onto rail cars or the draymen's horse-drawn wagons.

The arrival of the railroads improved Seattle's position as a regional port. More trade meant more jobs for the longshoremen, but nothing changed the back-breaking methods of moving cargo from ship, to shore, to

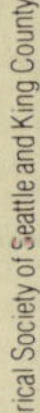

74

warehouse or to railroad cars or drays. Remnants of this era can be seen on the north side of Pier 56. There, the depressed railroad tracks on the narrow pier apron are still visible, and it is easy to imagine cargo being unloaded onto the wharf and moved by hand truck through the large side doors into the shed to await pickup by a teamster and his horse-drawn dray. Old rail sidings exist on many of the piers, especially Piers 54, 55, 57, 62, 63, and 64.

At the beginning of the twentieth century, some small technological improvements eased the longshoremen's work. They began to use slings made of stout rope nets attached to the ship's boom to hoist crates and other cargo out of the holds. The invention of the gas-powered engine also contributed to the mechanization of freight handling. In the 1920s, small gas-driven jitneys could speedily pull a chain of four-wheeled pallets stacked with goods through the transit sheds, and early fork-lift trucks could stack boxed cargoes. Even so, the longshoremen's job and the function of the finger piers changed very little.

The stevedores who handled cumbersome bulk goods were assisted by rapid advances in mechanization long before those who hauled break-bulk items. In the 1920s, the movement of commodities like grain and petroleum changed radically. Originally transported in

Pier Transit Sheds

Waterfront transit sheds—the name given to warehouses constructed on Elliott Bay piers—were built with the needs of cargo handling in mind. Most of them were completed at

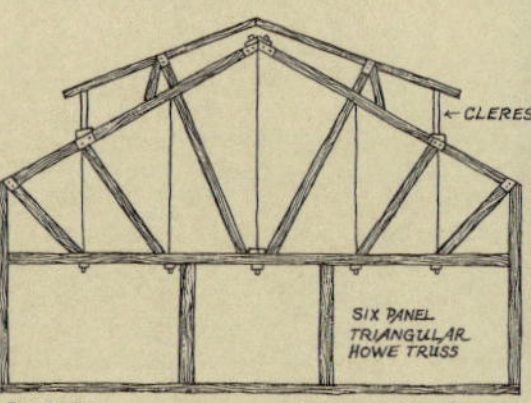

the turn of the century when the large, open floors allowed easy movement and storage of large volumes of cargo. Warehouse builders employed a variety of truss systems to distribute the vertical load to the side walls, thereby avoiding the need for columns or supports. Roof monitors, which look like smaller versions of the original shed piggybacked on the roof, were frequently used to provide inexpensive lighting and ventilation. Along the sides of the monitors are clerestory windows and louvered vents. Although working with similar requirements, each builder solved the problem in a slightly different way, as illustrated by the truss systems for Piers 57 and 59. In addition to the slight differences in form, the subtle effects of color, uneven settlement, and weathering on the piers and sheds give the Seattle waterfront its special character and patina.

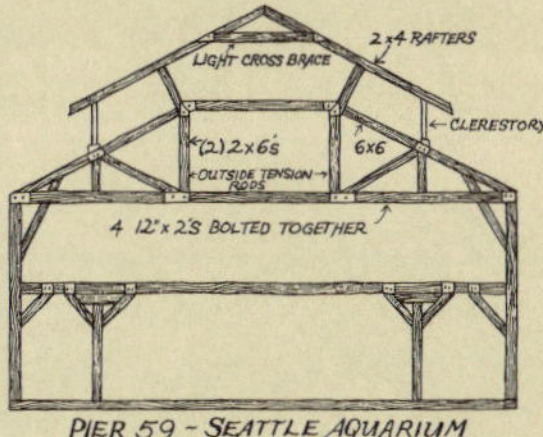

Electric tractor and trailers used in the 1920s.

bags, grain was now moved by air-blown tubes and suction devices and shipped in specially designed vessels. Petroleum, too, once shipped in barrels, began moving by tanker at the turn of the century.

It was not until World War II that pallets and fork-lift trucks were introduced as the first major stride in mechanizing the movement of break-bulk cargo. Cargoes were stacked on wooden or metal pallets measuring four by six feet, transferred as a single unit from ship to shore, and moved by fork lift to warehouses or other transfer points where the boxes often remained stored on a pallet. With machines aiding their labor, longshoremen were no longer merely beasts of burden. This simple change cut ship-loading and -unloading time in half, although moving cargo in and out of a ship could still take up to ten days.

Dockworkers use pallets and fork lifts to move cargo today. A good place to see this on the waterfront is at Pier 54, behind Ivar's. Other spots to observe some of the old cargo-handling techniques include Piers 20, 91, and 115. At the Fisher Mills on Harbor Island, flour must be loaded by hand for the Far East and other world ports that do not yet have modern facilities.

After World War II, changes were brewing that dramati-

Port of Seattle

cally affected the shape and function of the central waterfront. Intercity and interstate trucking began to compete with the railroads for cross-country freight hauling. The mechanization of bulk-commodity handling led to innovations in cargo-ship design. Larger, specially designed vessels required expanded facilities and handling equipment not available on the smaller finger piers. Some terminals, such as the Terminal 86 bulk-grain facility, were built to handle one specific type of commodity. There was also an increasing American demand for foreign-made products and an unprecedented growth in some of the world's trading nations. New port facilities were needed to accommodate these changes, and in the search for an appropriate site, the central waterfront

and the old finger piers were abandoned. High downtown land costs, shortage of back-up space for cargo storage, access and congestion problems, excessively deep water immediately offshore, and the outmoded finger piers were among the many reasons behind the demise of the central waterfront as the hub of Seattle's commerce.

The shift away from the old piers had already begun, but the death knell sounded in 1949, when the Alaska Steamship Company began using collapsible, reusable wooden "cribs" to consolidate loose cargo into single units on their runs between Seattle and Alaska. This innovation took hold in the late 1950s, when both Matson Lines and Sea-Land, two established shipping firms, began the large-scale use of containers, and by 1970 the Container Revolution had swept the shipping industry.

This new and versatile method of shipping cargo in preloaded boxes of uniform shapes and sizes suitable for overland transportation meant that break-bulk cargo no longer needed individual treatment. Whereas the old ship's sling held up to one ton of loose crates, a twenty-foot container now holds a seventeen-ton payload and a forty-foot container, thirty-three tons.[1] Containers can be lifted on and off a ship and stacked either in the hold or on deck. They can also be loaded on a truck chassis, treating it like a semitrailer, or they can as easily be secured on a rail flatcar.

With containers, ship-loading and -unloading efficiency has been increased five to ten times over conventional handling by pallet and fork-lift truck. It used to take five days to unload and reload 10,000 tons of cargo from the old vessels using forty to fifty men. It takes twenty men about seven hours to load and unload the same amount of cargo in containers. Now a ship can make twenty-two round trips per year on the Seattle-Hawaii run, as opposed to only twelve before.[2]

For its profound technological impacts on the shipping industry, containerization has been equated with other innovations such as the shift from sail to steam power that freed ships from the whims of

Nature's winds and the move from wood to steel hulls that increased ships' strength and, therefore, their size and carrying capacity. Accompanying the shift to containerization was an array of expensive facility requirements. From the Smith Tower, Pier 57, or several other vantage points along the waterfront, there is a good view of the Terminal 37/46 complex, one of Seattle's newest and largest container facilities. It is vastly different from the scene on the old waterfront.

The containers, basic elements of the new technology, are built to internationally established standards, allowing them to be moved through any container port in the world, from Amsterdam to Zanzibar. These sturdy steel boxes are usually 8 feet wide, 8 feet high, and 20 to 40 feet long,[3] but they come in assorted types to handle different cargoes. When a ship arrives at Terminal 46, the orange, 105-foot-high container crane, mounted on rails on the apron, lifts a container out of the ship and lowers it directly onto a truck chassis for storage in the yard or transport to its final destination. Some day soon, the colossal cranes may disappear from the waterfront. New technology may allow containers to slide into a ship's hold on large sheets, similar to the way bread is put into an oven.

Boxes stacked on wooden pallets and moved as one unit advanced cargo movement in the 1940s.

Historical Society of Seattle and King County

There are other methods of stacking and storing containers besides the method used at Terminal 46. At Terminal 18 on the northeast corner of Harbor Island, the crane unloads containers onto the apron. A straddle carrier, looking something like a spider on wheels, then picks up a container and stacks it in a row two and three containers high in the storage yard. Later another carrier will retrieve the stored container and load it onto a truck to be taken to the rail yards or to a final destination in the Seattle area. Terminal 25 and Terminal 37 use similar equipment but can store containers in larger and denser stacks.

Instead of the narrow pier aprons and transit sheds required in the old days, all this activity demands a large quantity of open backup space, called container yards, to accommodate the stored containers, trailers, chassis, cranes, gates, terminals, and offices. Ideally, each container-ship berth should have twenty to twenty-five acres of backup space. The industrial lands created out of the tideflats in the south harbor area were well suited to the development of container facilities and today there are approximately 300 acres of container yards serving fifteen berths in the south harbor area.[4]

The Miike Maru and the Liu Lin Hai

When the one-stack steamer, the *Miike Maru*, tied up at Schwabacher's Wharf on August 31, 1896, she was greeted by blaring whistles and much fanfare. The arrival of this ship, her hold brimming with tea, marked the beginning of regular shipping service between Seattle and the Orient. A contract between James Hill's Great Northern Railroad and Japan's Nippon Yusen Kaisha shipping line established Seattle as a major port for the Far East trade and opened the door for an immense volume of commerce between the two countries. Trade from the Orient surpassed all expectations, and soon millions of dollars of raw silk, tea, and other exotic goods poured across Seattle's docks.[1] Seattle had indeed become the Gateway to the Orient.

World War II and upheavals in China temporarily closed the door on Asian trade, but the resumption of trade with Japan and more recently with mainland China, along with growing trade with other Pacific Rim ports, has maintained Seattle's position as a preeminent port for East-West commerce. Once again a ship's arrival commemorated the event. On April 18, 1979, the *Liu Lin Hai* docked in Seattle at Pier 91. It was the first vessel from mainland China to land in a U.S. port in thirty years, and it marked the normalization of relations between the two powers. The *Liu Lin Hai* left Seattle for Shanghai loaded with 37,000 metric tons of Midwestern corn.[2]

Technology has replaced brawn at today's container terminals. Large, sophisticated pieces of equipment are operated by fewer, more highly trained longshoremen. Radio operators now orchestrate the complex activities in the container yards, directing the maneuvers of cranes, carriers, and trucks and keeping track of each and every container at all times. Even fewer longshoremen may be needed in the future — computers are expected to play a larger role conducting a variety of container-yard chores such as record keeping, loading and unloading, and warehouse and berth scheduling. Phoenician dockworkers would not recognize the waterfront that has emerged since the Container Revolution

Ever since the first cargo of sawn logs left Seattle for San Francisco, Elliott Bay has been dedicated to moving freight between Seattle and the world's ports of call. Although the central waterfront was for years the hub of all this commerce, changing shipping technology has helped shift the focus to other parts of the harbor. Today all the container activity takes place in the south harbor, where large orange cranes symbolize the new shipping era that has witnessed Seattle's emergence as one of the nation's largest container ports.

Today container cranes dominate the working waterfront.

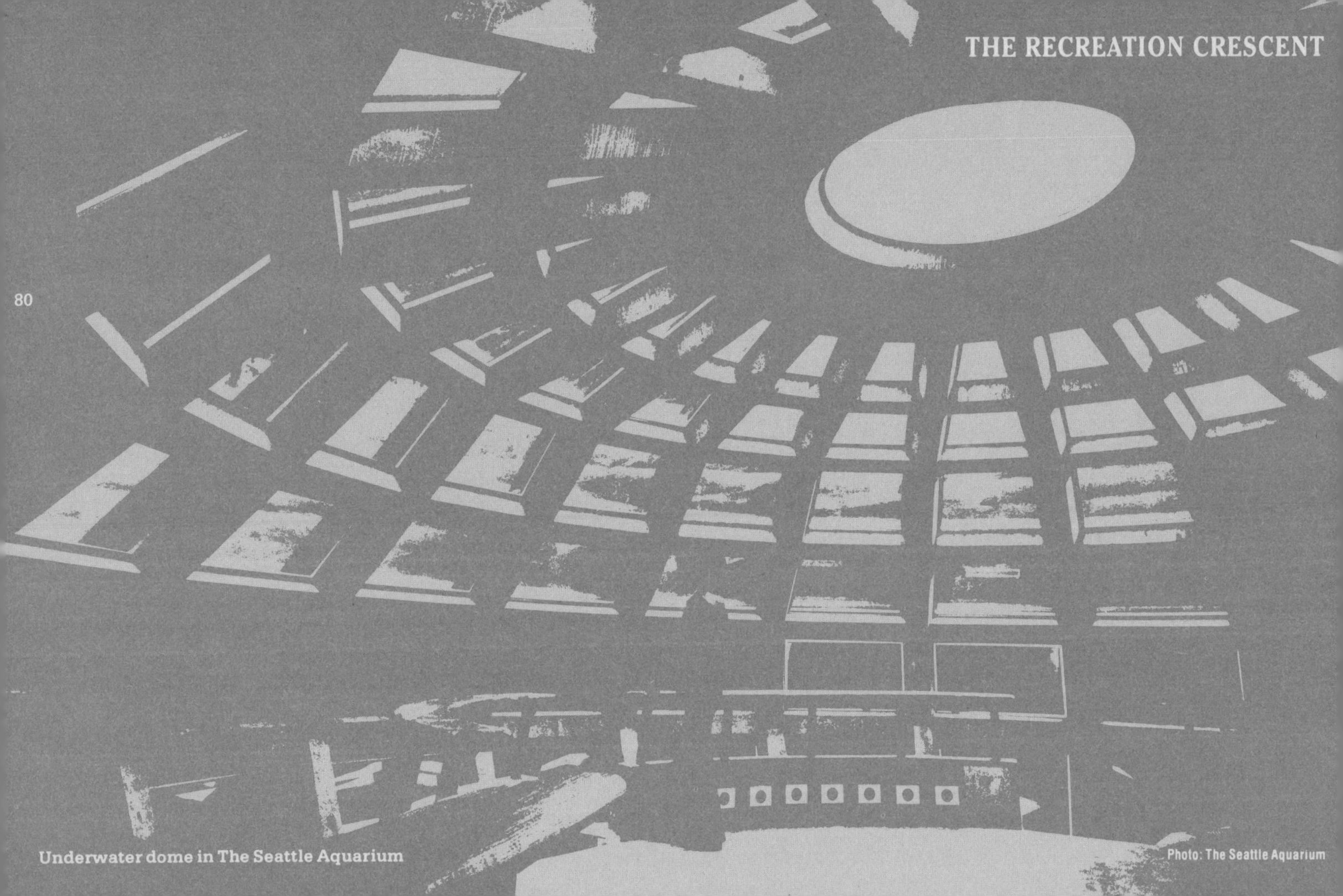

Underwater dome in The Seattle Aquarium

Photo: The Seattle Aquarium

Revitalizing the Central Waterfront

Early-day recreation on Elliott Bay included swimming, sport fishing, and especially boating, whether that meant rowing, racing, or recreational cruising. Hardly anyone, however, thought of recreation as the major use of Seattle's central waterfront in those days when the growing city needed all the available land there for marine commerce and industry. What is today a part of Seattle's Entertainment Crescent had rather sporadic beginnings.

Seattle's first improved bathing beach, Jensen's, opened in 1877 between Pike and Union streets, near where the Seattle Aquarium is today. Jensen's had twelve bathhouses where suits and towels could be rented.[1] A favorite early swimming hole for Seattle youngsters was a sandy beach north of Columbia Street.

The early settlers used the bay for sport fishing as is still done today at the Public Fishing Piers 57 and 86. A seventy-five-pound halibut was caught from Yesler's Wharf in 1876. In 1882 the first shad was caught in the harbor, and the first barracuda on record in Elliott Bay was caught in 1886.[2]

In July 1872, Seattle's first boat club was organized, and invitations were sent to Olympia and Victoria for races on Elliott Bay. The first organized regatta did not take place until July 1875, when six sailboats raced on the bay.[3]

In the 1880s, however, Budlong's Boathouse, near where the ferry terminal is today, was a center of aquatic activity. Budlong was a first-class boatbuilder and always had rowboats, cat boats, and sloops for rent. In those days, most sailboat racing took place on a fifteen-mile, triangular course in Elliott Bay.[4] In 1886 the Puget Sound Yacht Club was established at Budlong's Boathouse, and the club's first cup race was held in August 1886.[5] The Great Fire of 1889, which razed almost all of Seattle's waterfront buildings, also took Budlong's, and the boathouse was never rebuilt.

Starting in 1894, another club, the Elliott Bay Yacht Club, operated from the Brighton Boathouse further north at the foot of Battery Street. By 1903 most of the yachts and small craft of the city were moored there, and it was the site of festivities and a major regatta during the Alaska-Yukon-Pacific Exposition in 1909. The Elliott Bay Yacht Club was eventually consolidated with the Seattle Yacht Club which operated a clubhouse near the West Seattle Ferry Dock starting in 1892.[6]

Besides its use for swimming, fishing, and pleasure boating, the downtown waterfront has been a central departure point for recreational cruises since the days of the Mosquito Fleet. Because few people owned cars or boats in those days, a favorite holiday activity was an excursion on a fleet steamer. One popular trip was on the West Seattle Ferry to Luna Park on Duwamish Head. Luna Park, an amusement park patterned after Coney Island, featured a salt-water swimming pool and rides. Realtors selling property in West Seattle provided free transportation on the ferry.

Excursions on the Sound were a part of every holiday, and on such gala occasions, many steamers carried bands. One became famous for its steam calliope, another for its nickelodeon.

Budlong's Boathouse, headquarters for
the Puget Sound Yacht Club in the
1880s.

*On quiet passages of the
Sound, a holiday often began
with the faint strains of dis-
tant music.*[7]

As far back as 1903,
Seattleites began to want a
formal park on the downtown
waterfront. In that year, the
Olmsted Brothers, nationally
known landscape architects,
proposed a small harbor
park to be located either at
the foot of Battery Street,
where the Brighton Boat-
house was then, or at the foot
of Denny Way, where Myrtle
Edwards Park is today. The
park was to feature a pleasure pier for boat moorage
and a bulkhead terrace area.
A sandy beach for bathers
was also suggested, but
contamination from sewage
was already beginning to be
a concern. Although the
Olmsteds' recommendations
formed the basis for Seattle's
park system, their waterfront
park was never developed.

Brighton Boathouse at the turn of the century.

Another unrealized plan proposed two huge marinas on the central waterfront for both the Mosquito Fleet and private pleasure boats. This plan was envisioned in 1911 by Virgil Bogue, Seattle's first city planner. Seattle voters rejected the idea in the 1912 election, however, largely because of adverse publicity.

Three years later in 1915, Seattle's first waterfront park, with a solarium, salt-water pool, and children's play area, was finally developed by the Port of Seattle on the roof of their Bell Street terminal. Originally designed as a place where mothers could leave their children while shopping at the nearby Pike Place Market, the park came to be used most by sailors and their Pike Street companions and was closed in the 1920s.[8]

From the 1920s until about 1960, the waterfront's potential for tourist and recreational activity was largely ignored. However, some local entrepreneurs did recognize the commercial potential in the central waterfront. A few tourist-oriented businesses—such as Ye Olde Curiosity Shop, first located on the waterfront in 1899, and Ivar's Acres of Clams, which opened in 1938— predated the recent emergence of the central waterfront as part of Seattle's Entertainment Crescent. Throughout this time, Colman Dock, later Colman Ferry Terminal, remained a mecca for tourists because boat cruises on Puget Sound have always been popular. Today this dock is the site of the Washington State Ferries terminal.

By the time of the Seattle World's Fair in 1962, most industrial activities had shifted to the area south of the central waterfront, and tourism and recreation began to gain momentum. During the World's Fair, the floating hotels along the waterfront indicated a resurgence of interest in the area. The city expected a shortage of hotel space, and three ships were brought to the Elliott Bay waterfront to serve as floating hotels: the S.S. *Acapulco* berthed alongside Pier 70, the *Catala* moored at Pier 58, and the *Dominion Monarch* at Pier 50. In addition to the hotels, there was a floating restaurant on the *Skagit*

Sunday Mosquito Fleet excursions were a popular pastime.

Puget Sound Maritime Historical Society, Williamson Collection

Belle, berthed at Pier 51. The expectations proved overly optimistic, however, and the floating hotels lost money and were gone by the time the World's Fair was over. Only one hotel remains on the waterfront today, the Edge-water Inn at Pier 67, which was built at the time of the World's Fair.

Although it is unlikely that more hotels will be built on the central waterfront, the surge of tourism and recreation begun in the 1960s continues today. In the 1970s, several parks were developed that fulfilled long-time dreams of early planners such as the Olmsted Brothers and Virgil Bogue. Waterfront Park opened in 1974 at Piers 57 and 58,

Seattle's Early Aquariums

The first recorded marine exhibit in Seattle occurred in 1908, when a dead whale washed ashore at Luna Park in West Seattle, but it did not last long since the whale was soon pulled out into Elliott Bay because of its stench. The next fish exhibit began in 1917, with a frozen, 331-pound halibut display in the hall of a cold-storage plant at the Spokane Street Terminal. Fishermen brought unusual fish from all over the world, and in 1918 an exhibit touted as the "only frozen fish exhibit in the U.S. and Canada"[1] opened to the public. By 1936 there were 300 frozen fish, including a sunfish, luna fish, and starfish in the exhibit. It finally closed in 1956.

A deep-sea aquarium was established for a

short time at the West Seattle Boat House in the late 1930s, and in 1938 Ivar Haglund built an aquarium at the end of Pier 3, now Pier 54, in conjunction with his restaurant. In 1945, his restaurant having grown in popularity, Ivar converted the aquarium space to dining area. In 1949, bemoaning the loss of Ivar's aquarium, the Seattle Harbor Tours ticket office tried to fill the gap by exhibiting "the world's smallest public aquarium": a one-gallon jar containing various interesting bits of sea life, the most popular of which was a barnacle known as Old Barney.[2]

At the time of the Seattle World's Fair in 1962, Ted Griffin, a skin-diver and businessman, built an aquarium at Pier 56. The most famous exhibit at Griffin's aquarium was Namu, a killer whale from the waters off

The dedication ceremony in 1915 for the Port of Seattle's rooftop park.

known as Schwabacher's Wharf during the Gold Rush days. The City and the Port of Seattle developed two contiguous parks north of Pier 70, Myrtle Edwards Park and Elliott Bay Park, which opened in July 1976. Part of the shoreline there was landfill dumped during the construction of Interstate 5 through Seattle.

From its modest beginnings, the central waterfront has grown to provide a vast array of recreational activities, and today about 10,000 people visit the area daily in summer. Seattle's award-winning Aquarium, which opened in 1977, is a popular regional attraction. It offers a variety of fine educational displays about marine life, including corridors exhibiting Puget Sound sea life, an underwater viewing dome, and live sea otters and seals. There is jogging and bicycling year-around along the paths at Elliott Bay Park. Tourists and Seattleites alike can watch ships entering the harbor and look south to view the huge container terminals on Harbor Island while enjoying a picnic on Pier 57. Public fishing has always been possible along the central waterfront, and the newly dedicated Pier 86, jointly developed by the Port of Seattle and the State Department of Fisheries, now provides space for 500 anglers.

86

The waterfront along Alaskan Way, from Pier 70's forty shops and restaurants to the Port of Seattle's Alaska Square Park at Pier 48, is a busy pedestrian promenade. There are import shops, boutiques, marine-supply outlets, and shoreside fish-and-chips stands. All kinds of boat rides appeal to tourists and local residents alike — harbor tours, ferries across Puget Sound, a steamship to Victoria, and a ferry trip up the Inside Passage to Alaska. There is even a boat tour to Blake Island which leaves from Pier 56 and features Native American dancing and a salmon bake. Historic waterfront trolleys brought from Australia will soon run along Alaskan Way, providing easy access between Pier 48 and Pier 70. The Pike Street Hillclimb connects the waterfront with the nearby Pike Place Market, one of Seattle's

most popular attractions and a good place for views of Elliott Bay.

Every year the local celebrations of Maritime Week in May and Seafair in July feature activities such as boat parades and races as well as waterfront tours. Self-guided walking tours can be taken at any time of the year by following the historical plaque anchors located along the waterfront and indicated on

British Columbia. Griffin's aquarium closed in 1976, when a municipal aquarium was constructed. Funded by the 1968 Forward Thrust Bond Issue, the present-

day Seattle Aquarium at Pier 59 opened in 1977. The Aquarium is a major attraction on the waterfront, drawing more than 700,000 visitors in 1980 alone.

the map at the end of this book. In the summer, the waterfront has a festive atmosphere signaled by the colorful, bright banners that wave in the wind along Alaskan Way.

There is every indication that the era of waterfront redevelopment is only beginning and that tourism and recreation will continue to thrive on the central waterfront. At least a half-dozen projects now in the planning stages emphasize its function as an entertainment, recreation, and retail center. In addition to several retail shopping arcades proposed on the piers, a large waterfront complex is planned between First Avenue and the Alaskan Way Viaduct. A mixed residential, retail, and office project, possibly including moorage space, is envisioned at the Union Oil Dock. The waterfront, once the economic lifeblood of Seattle as a center for commerce and transportation, is now becoming an economic boon as a mecca for recreation and tourism.

Throughout its history, Seattle's waterfront, as a link between the land and the sea, has been a magnet for a diverse assortment of activity. In fact, the waterfront is the raison d'être for Seattle itself. The city was founded on Elliott Bay because of its fine natural harbor, where the pioneers envisioned a center for trade and industry on Puget Sound, yet the waterfront also has a special magic that draws people to it for recreation and relaxation. A bird's-eye view of Elliott Bay on almost any day in the past 130 years would show the rich tapestry created by this diverse activity — ships and trains, fishermen, stevedores, and picnickers filling the waterfront along a crescent-shaped bay.

When water was the only link among the communities on Puget Sound, Seattle's central position and its ambitious citizens combined to establish the city as the focal point of the region and to develop a wide array of business enterprises. From the time when Henry Yesler built his first wharf, through the heyday of the Mosquito Fleet, the waterfront was dominated by commerce, transportation, and industry, yet there was still room for recreational activities such as sport fishing and early yacht races. Although commercial concerns were paramount, the city was small enough that this diverse use of the harbor was concentrated in one area, the central waterfront.

Trade, industry, and recreation still coexist along Elliott Bay today, but their distribution has shifted, and with this shift the emphasis on the central waterfront has changed. Industry and port activity have moved to the north and south, where there is adequate backup space for modern cargo-handling equipment and storage. While the sawtooth pier configuration along the central waterfront looks much as it did at the turn of the century, the piers themselves have been adapted for new uses, and they now house recreational activities such as shopping arcades, restaurants, and parks. Because Elliott Bay has been adaptable to changing needs, Seattle has been able to keep up with the times in marine commerce as well as to attract the leisure-time activities that have spearheaded the redevelopment of the central waterfront.

With its renaissance as an entertainment center today, the central waterfront has entered a new era, but Elliott Bay continues to be a diverse hub of activity. It is home to shipbuilding, cargo movement, public fishing, dining, shopping, and a large ferry system. The harbor is still a gateway for travelers, as it was during the Gold Rush and in the prime of the Mosquito Fleet. The waterfront is both Seattle's leading edge and its lifeblood, a taking-off point and a center of commerce and recreation. Playing a vital role in Seattle's development as the preeminent city of the Northwest, the waterfront is also a unique and colorful district in its own right, with a rich history and a promising future.

REFERENCE NOTES

1. **SEATTLE'S WATERFRONT: THE LEADING EDGE OF A CHANGING CITY**
   1. Murray Morgan, *Skid Road*, p. 3.

2. **THE DUWAMISH PEOPLE: FIRST TO SETTLE ON ELLIOTT BAY**
   1. Interview with David Buerge, historian of the Duwamish people, 5 February 1981.
   2. David Buerge, "Seattle 3000 B.C.–1851 A.D."
   3. Clarence B. Bagley, *History of King County*, p. 124.
   4. Buerge, "Seattle 3000 B.C.–1851 A.D."
   5. Seattle Historical Society, *Seattle Century*, p. 70.
   6. According to David Buerge, the Duwamish are in the process of appealing in order to establish themselves as a legally recognized tribe. If they are recognized as a political entity, they will then qualify for Indian fishing rights under the Boldt decision.
   7. Chief Sealth's address delivered at the signing of the Point Elliott Treaty in 1855. In Buerge, "Seattle 3000 B.C.–1851 A.D."

HOW SEATTLE GOT ITS NAME
   1. Seattle Historical Society, *Seattle Century*, p. 105.

3. **TIDEFLATS TO MODERN HARBOR: SHAPING SEATTLE'S WATERFRONT**
   1. Makers, *Alaskan Way Seawall and Promenade Guideplan.*
   2. Arthur H. Dimock, "Preparing the Groundwork for a City: The Regrading of Seattle, Washington," Paper No. 1669, American Society of Civil Engineers (Reprinted from *Transactions*, vol. 92, 1928, pp. 717–18); Lucille McDonald, "Seattle's 'Made Land'."
   3. McDonald, "Seattle's 'Made Land'."
   4. *Daily Pacific Tribune*, 21 June 1875. In John Robert Finger, *Henry L. Yesler's Seattle Years 1852–1892*, p. 301.
   5. McDonald, "Seattle's 'Made Land'."
   6. Paul Benoit, "The Man-Induced Topographic Change of Seattle's Elliott Bay Shoreline from 1852 to 1930 as an Early Form of Coastal Resource Use and Management," p. 37.
   7. R. H. Thomson, *That Man Thomson*, ed. Grant H. Redford (Seattle: University of Washington Press, 1950), p. 14.
   8. Dimock, "Preparing the Groundwork," p. 729; R. M. Overstreet, "Seattle's Regrades—A Giant Accomplishment," *Argus*, 18 December 1909; Benoit, "Man-Induced Topographic Change," p. 55.
   9. "Cotterill Explodes Seawall Bubble," *Seattle Times*, 1 January 1910.
   10. Susan MacDonald, "Railroad Avenue and the Seawall, Seattle's Long-Time Vexation," *Port of Seattle Reporter*, January 1972, p. 3.

SUNKEN SHIPS ALONG SEATTLE'S WATERFRONT
   1. Gordon R. Newell, *Ships of the Inland Sea*, p. 80; David Suffia, "A Lot of History Lies Under Seattle's Waterfront," *Seattle Times*, 6 July 1975; J. Willis Sayre, *The Early Waterfront of Seattle*, pp. 19–20; Myra L. Phelps, *Public Works in Seattle, A Narrative History, The Engineering Department 1875–1975*, p. 70; "Skagit Belle Is Still a Scenic Blot," *Seattle Times*, 11 June 1968.

"GET THE TIDELAND HABIT IT WILL MAKE MONEY WHILE YOU SLEEP."
   1. Charles B. Bussell, *Tide Lands, Their Story*, n. pag.
   2. Thomas Burke Papers, letter to Miss Carrie L. Allen, University of Washington Libraries Manuscripts Collection, 1 May 1888. In Benoit, "Man-Induced Topographic Change," p. 23.
   3. Bussell, *Tide Lands, Their Story*, n. pag.

4. **YESLER'S WHARF: BIRTHPLACE OF COMMERCE AND INDUSTRY**
   1. *Daily Pacific Tribune*, 25 November 1876.
   2. *Seattle Weekly Intelligencer*, 3 July 1875.
   3. John Robert Finger, *Henry L. Yesler's Seattle Years 1852–1892*, p. 300.
   4. Ibid., p. 132.
   5. Ibid., p. 305.

TEREDOS!
   1. Edward F. Ricketts and Jack Calvin, *Between Pacific Tides*, 4th ed. rev. Joel W. Hedgpeth (Stanford: Stanford University

Press, 1968), p. 360.

THE *ELIZA ANDERSON*
DOCKS AT YESLER'S WHARF
1. Gordon R. Newell, *Ships of the Inland Sea*, p. 23.

5. MOSQUITO FLEET TO FERRY FLEET: TRANSPORTATION HUB ON ELLIOTT BAY
1. Interview with Robert Leithead, maritime historian, 17 March 1981.
2. Clarence B. Bagley, "Ships on Puget Sound," *Seattle Times*, 27 December 1903.
3. *Seattle Gazette*, 20 August 1864. In Roland Carey, *The Steamboat Landing on Elliott Bay*, p. 16.
4. Alexander Norbert MacDonald, *Seattle's Economic Development 1880–1910*, p. 32.
5. J. Willis Sayre, *The Early Waterfront of Seattle*, p. 12.
6. Gordon R. Newell, *Ships of the Inland Sea*, p. 126.
7. Captain Torger Birkeland, *Echoes of Puget Sound*, pp. 122–23.
8. Newell, *Inland Sea*, p. 113.
9. Carey, *Steamboat Landing*, p. 61.
10. Gordon R. Newell, ed., *The H. W. McCurdy Marine History of the Pacific Northwest*, p. 437.
11. Birkeland, *Puget Sound*, p. 129.

THE HISTORY OF COLMAN DOCK
1. H. Cole Estep, "New Colman Dock at Seattle," p. 38.
2. Ibid., p. 38.

6. THE RAILROADS: BARRICADING THE WATERFRONT
1. Cornelius H. Hanford, *Seattle and Environs 1852–1924*, p. 189.
2. Padraic Burke, *A History of the Port of Seattle*, p. 23.
3. Ibid., p. 23.
4. Jack Heise, "Tunnel under City Was Early Seattle Problem," *Seattle Star*, 26 January 1933.
5. Great Northern Railway Company, Public Relations Department, "Seattle and the Great Northern Railway," n.d., p. 11.
6. "Seattle Tunnel Now 50 Years Old," *Seattle Times*, 30 January 1955.
7. Great Northern Railway Company, "Seattle and the Great Northern Railway," p. 12.
8. *Report of Seattle Terminal Survey Committee to Chamber of Commerce and Commercial Club on Seattle Rail and Water Terminals and Harbor Improvements*, R. A. Ballinger, Chairman (Seattle), April 1918, p. 10.
9. Ibid., pp. 10–11.

SILK TRAINS
1. George Foster, "There Was Another Ship, Back in 1896," *Seattle Post-Intelligencer*, 18 April 1979.
2. Lucille McDonald, "When the Last Silk Train Rushed Out of Seattle"; interview with Frederick W. Short, Media Services Manager, Port of Seattle, March 1981.

THE ARRIVAL OF THE GREAT NORTHERN
1. Great Northern Railway Company, "Seattle and the Great Northern Railway," p. 6.

7. GOLD RUSH: SEATTLE, GATEWAY TO ALASKA
1. Editorial, *Seattle Post-Intelligencer*, 20 July 1897.
2. "Tourists to Hike Old Trail," *Seattle Times*, 8 April 1962.
3. Pierre Berton, *The Klondike Fever*, p. 107.
4. Ibid., p. 112.
5. David and Judie Clarridge, "A Ton of Gold," p. 8.
6. Berton, *Klondike Fever*, pp. 124–25.
7. Alexander Norbert MacDonald, *Seattle's Economic Development 1880–1910*, p. 195.
8. Berton, *Klondike Fever*, p. 125.
9. Ibid., p. 434.

THE *ELIZA ANDERSON'S* LAST VOYAGE
1. The information presented in this fictitious note is based on material from Berton, *Klondike Fever*, pp. 141–45.

8. WATERFRONT PIERS: THE SAWTOOTH LOOK OF ELLIOTT BAY
1. Roger Sale, *Seattle, Past to Present*, p. 50. Murray Morgan in *Skid Road*, p. 109, indicates a total of twenty-five blocks were burned.
2. *Speidel's Seattle Guide*, October 3–10, 1980, p. 23.
3. George F. Cotterill. "Report of State Agent on Re-Adjustment of Seattle Tide Lands Replat," pp. 59–63.

THE SEATTLE FIRE
1. Sale, *Seattle*, pp. 50–51; Morgan, *Skid Road*, pp. 103–11.

9. **SHIPBUILDING:** THE UPS AND DOWNS OF A MAJOR WATERFRONT INDUSTRY

1. "Puget Sound Record in Early Shipbuilding," *Railway and Marine News*, p. 26.
2. Gordon R. Newell, *Ships of the Inland Sea*, p. 34.
3. Museum of History and Industry Photo Collection, Shipbuilding, *George E. Starr* Photo #2429.
4. Joe Williamson and Jim Gibbs, *Maritime Memories of Puget Sound*, p. 159.
5. Cornelius Hanford, *Seattle and Environs 1852–1924*, p. 275.
6. Ibid., pp. 356–59; interview with J. J. Dillon, maritime historian, February 1981.
7. Hanford, *Seattle and Environs*, p. 356.
8. Gordon R. Newell, ed., *The H. W. McCurdy Marine History of the Pacific Northwest*, p. 478.
9. Interview with H. W. McCurdy, April 1981.
10. Newell, *McCurdy Marine History*, pp. 486–506.

THE SPEED DEMONS OF WORLD WAR I

1. "Skinner & Eddy Corporation Sets New Record," *Railway and Marine News*, p. 36.
2. Edgar I. Stewart, *Washington Northwest Frontier*, vol. 2, (New York: Lewis Historical Publishing Company, Inc.), p. 232.

10. **CARGO HANDLING:** OF HAND TRUCKS, FORK LIFTS, AND CONTAINERS

1. Victoria Yund, "Seattle: Gateway to the Orient," *Port of Seattle Reporter*, Fall 1980, p. 12.
2. Mees and Hope and Zoonen Assurantien, *Container Transport*, Amsterdam, 1967, pp. 9–10.
3. Yund, "Gateway to Orient"; interview with Paul Chilcote, Senior Trade Analyst, Port of Seattle, February 1981.
4. Port of Seattle, *Facilities Handbook*, January 1980; interview with Frederick W. Short, Media Services Manager, Port of Seattle, April 1981.

THE *MIIKE MARU* AND THE *LIU LIN HAI*

1. Padraic Burke, *A History of the Port of Seattle*, p. 10; Alexander Norbert MacDonald, *Seattle's Economic Development 1880–1910*, pp. 149–51.
2. *"Liu Lin Hai* calls on the Port of Seattle," *Port of Seattle Reporter*, Spring 1980, p. 18; George Foster, "There Was Another Ship, Back in 1896," *Seattle Post-Intelligencer*, 18 April 1979.

11. **THE RECREATION CRESCENT:** REVITALIZING THE CENTRAL WATERFRONT

1. J. Willis Sayre, *The Early Waterfront of Seattle*, p. 16.
2. Ibid., p. 17.
3. Seattle Historical Society, *Seattle Century*, p. 86.
4. Frank R. Atkins, "Life in Seattle Before the Big Fire Recalled," *Seattle Star*, 14 August 1937.
5. Seattle Historical Society, *Seattle Century*, p. 86.
6. Ibid., p. 68.
7. Roland Carey, *The Sound of Steamers*, p. 4.
8. Padraic Burke, *A History of the Port of Seattle*, pp. 43–44.

SEATTLE'S EARLY AQUARIUMS

1. Don Sherwood, "Waterfront Park/Aquarium," in "Interpretive Essays of the Histories of Seattle's Parks and Playgrounds," p. 4.
2. Ibid., p. 5.

BIBLIOGRAPHY

Bagley, Clarence B. *History of King County*. Chicago-Seattle: The S. J. Clarke Publishing Company, 1929.

Benoit, Paul. "The Man-Induced Topographic Change of Seattle's Elliott Bay Shoreline from 1852 to 1930 as an Early Form of Coastal Resource Use and Management." Master's report, Marine Affairs, University of Washington, 1979.

Berton, Pierre. *The Klondike Fever: The Life and Death of the Last Great Gold Rush*. New York: Alfred A. Knopf, 1958.

Birkeland, Captain Torger. *Echoes of Puget Sound: Fifty Years of Logging and Steamboating*. Caldwell, Idaho: Caxton Printers, 1960.

Buerge, David. "Seattle 3000 B.C. — 1851 A.D." *The Weekly*. 17 December 1980.

Burke, Padraic. *A History of the Port of Seattle*. Seattle: Port of Seattle, 1976.

Bussell, Charles B. *Tide Lands, Their Story*. Northwest Collection, University of Washington Libraries, Seattle, n.d.

Carefoot, Thomas. *Pacific Seashores: A Guide to Intertidal Ecology*. Seattle: University of Washington Press, 1977.

Carey, Roland. *The Sound of Steamers*. Seattle: Alderbrook Publishing Company, 1965.

Carey, Roland. *The Steamboat Landing on Elliott Bay*. Seattle: Alderbrook Publishing Company, 1970.

Chasan, Daniel. *The Water Link: A History of Puget Sound as a Resource*. Seattle: Washington Sea Grant, forthcoming.

Clarridge, David and Judie. "A Ton of Gold: The Seattle Gold Rush, 1897–1898." Unpublished manuscript, 1972.

Cotterill, George. "Report of State Agent on Re-Adjustment of Seattle Tide Lands Replat." *Sixth Biennial Report to the Commissioner of Public Lands*, 1 December 1900.

Estep, H. Cole. "New Colman Dock at Seattle." *The Marine Review*, December 1908, pp. 38–42.

Finger, John Robert. *Henry L. Yesler's Seattle Years 1852–1892*. Ph.D. dissertation, University of Washington, 1968.

Haeberlin, Hermann, and **Erna Gunther.** *The Indians of Puget Sound*. Seattle: University of Washington Press, 1930.

Hanford, Cornelius H. *Seattle and Environs 1852–1924*, vol. 1. Seattle: Pioneer Historical Publishing Company, 1924.

Hines, J. S. "Seattle, the 'Queen City'." *Pacific Marine Review*, July 1918, pp. 88–127.

Kozloff, Eugene N. *Seashore Life of Puget Sound, the Strait of Georgia, and the San Juan Archipelago*.

Seattle: University of Washington Press, 1973.

MacDonald, Alexander Norbert. *Seattle's Economic Development, 1880–1910*. Ph.D. dissertation, University of Washington, 1959.

McDonald, Lucille. "Seattle's 'Made Land'." *Seattle Times*, 27 December 1942.

McDonald, Lucille. "When the Last Silk Train Rushed Out of Seattle." *Seattle Times*, 10 March 1968.

Makers. *Alaskan Way Seawall and Promenade Guideplan, Seattle Central Waterfront*. Department of Engineering and Department of Community Development, 30 October 1979.

Morgan, Murray. *Skid Road: An Informal Portrait of Seattle*. Sausalito, California: Comstock Editions, Inc., 1978.

Newell, Gordon R., ed. *The H. W. McCurdy Marine History of the Pacific Northwest*. Seattle: Superior Publishing Company, 1965.

Newell, Gordon R. *Ships of the Inland Sea*. Portland: Binfords and Mort, 1960.

Phelps, Myra L. *Public Works in Seattle, A Narrative History, The Engineering Department, 1875–1975*. Seattle: Seattle Engineering Department, 1978.

Railway and Marine News, vol. 14, no. 12 (December 1916), pp. 17–39.

Sale, Roger. *Seattle, Past to Present*. Seattle: University of Washington Press, 1976.

Sayre, J. Willis. *The Early Waterfront of Seattle*. Seattle: J. W. Sayre, 1937.

Seattle Department of Community Development and **Rockrise Odermatt Mountjoy Amis.** *Seattle Central Waterfront, 1968–1971: A Comprehensive Plan for Its Future Development*. Seattle: City of Seattle, 1971.

Seattle Historical Society Research Committee. *Seattle Century*. Seattle: Superior Publishing Company, 1952.

Sherwood, Donald N. "Interpretive Essays of the Histories of Seattle's Parks and Playgrounds." Unpublished manuscript, 1977.

Shrader, Grahame F. *The Black Ball Line, 1929–1951*. Edmonds, Washington: Edmonds Printing Company, 1980.

Swensson, Anne B. "A Brief History of Seattle's South-Central Waterfront (Pier 42 and Environs)." Unpublished manuscript for the Port of Seattle, 1977.

Williamson, Joe, and **Jim Gibbs.** *Maritime Memories of Puget Sound*. Seattle: Superior Publishing Company, 1976.

← TO BAINBRIDGE ISLAND

PUGET SOUND

PIERS 90-91

GUIDEMAP

SEATTLE

CENTRAL
WATERFRONT

ELLIOTT BAY

EAST
WATERWAY

WEST
SEATTLE

HARBOR
ISLAND

WEST
WATERWAY

DUWAMISH
RIVER

Guidemap

Walk the pier-side of Alaskan Way between Piers 48 and 70, about one mile, and note

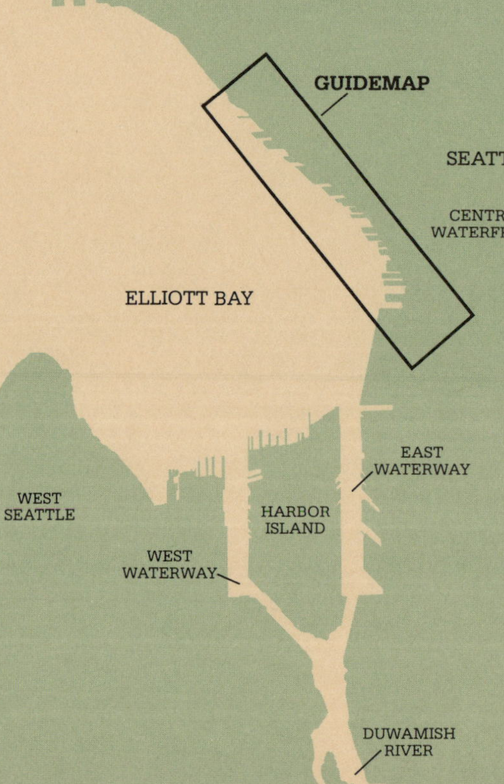 Historic Plaques

Historic Sites

and today's attractions as well. Key sites are described above the map.

For excellent harbor views visit the upper deck of the Ferry Terminal at Pier 52, or the outer ends of Pier 57 or Pier 70.

SCALE IN MILES

0   0.25   0.5   1 mile

S.S. *Portland* In July 1897, the *Portland* arrived at Schwabacher's Wharf carrying the "ton of gold" that started the stampede to the Klondike.

Aquarium/Pier 59 The location of today's Aquarium was once the site of coal bunkers whose pilings were destroyed by teredos (wood-boring worms) in the 1870s.

Piers 62 and 63 Once known as the Gaffney Dock and the Virginia Street Dock, these old piers were operated by Puget Sound Freight Lines until recently. (Photo)

North Portal of Railroad Tunnel From 1903 to 1905, the Great Northern and the Northern Pacific railroads built this tunnel to permit rail traffic to move through the city yet keep the waterfront open for commerce. (Photo)

J.F.T. Mitchell Shipyard J.F.T. Mitchell constructed the famous *George E. Starr* at his shipyard in the late 1870s and 1880s.

Brighton Boathouse The Brighton Boathouse was the headquarters for the Elliott Bay Yacht Club around the turn of the century.

Pier 70/Ainsworth-Dunn Dock Built from 1901 to 1902, today's popular shop and restaurant arcade, Pier 70, has led many different lives, having served as a salmon cannery, the headquarters for the Blue Funnel and Hamburg American Steamship lines, and a warehouse for the Liquor Control Board during World War II.

Pier 91/Smith Cove In the early part of this century, silk trains loaded precious cargo here at the "longest pier in the world." A navy base from World War II until 1976, Smith Cove has since then been a major port pier for automobiles, fruit, seafood, and general cargo.

The *Nebraska* The battleship *Nebraska,* Seattle's greatest shipbuilding achievement, slid down the ways of Moran Brothers shipyard on October 7, 1904. The pioneering Moran yard operated here between 1889 and 1906.

Ballast Island Years of dumping ships' ballast at the foot of Washington Street created Ballast Island, used as a camping ground by the Indian people in the 1880s and 1890s.

The *Idaho* Between 1900 and 1909, Dr. Alexander De Soto operated the Wayside Mission Hospital as a haven of comfort for Seattle's indigent in the old sidewheel steamer *Idaho,* moored here.

Pioneer Square This is the birthplace of Seattle. The Duwamish Indian village of Djidjila'letch, or "little crossing over place," stood here, and Henry Yesler later built his first sawmill on this spot. The Pioneer Building, erected by Yesler in 1889, commemorates his career.

Skid Road Yesler Way was where the term Skid Road originated, so named because logs were skidded down to Yesler's Mill over a track constructed of short logs laid across the roadbed.

Yesler's Mill Seattle's first industries — lumber, coal, flour — all had beginnings on Yesler's Wharf, built near here in 1854. (Photo)

Battle of Seattle This was the scene of the famous skirmish between the Indian people and the settlers on January 26, 1856. Anchored off shore, the U.S. sloop of war, the *Decatur,* protected the settlement by firing on the attackers and frightening them into retreat.

The *Windward* Beneath the grassy lot lies the remains of the bark *Windward.* Beached here in 1875, it is now embedded in shoreline landfill.

Pier 51/Ye Olde Curiosity Shop A waterfront institution since 1899, the shop was located on Colman Dock for sixty years before moving to Pier 51 in 1963.

Pier 52/Colman Dock Colman Dock was the focal point of the Mosquito Fleet for many years. Originally built around 1882, it was rebuilt several times before it was demolished to create the present ferry terminal in 1964. A new and even larger terminal is planned. (Photo)

Budlong's Boathouse Budlong's was the home base of the city's first formal pleasure boating organization, the Puget Sound Yacht Club, in the 1880s.

Grand Trunk Dock One of the major docks servicing the Mosquito Fleet and later the Black Ball Line, the Grand Trunk Pacific Dock was the Pacific Coast's largest modern structure when it opened here in 1910. After a fire on July 30, 1914, it was rebuilt and in use until the early 1960s. (Photo)

Fire Station No. 5 Dedicated in 1963, the present building resembles the original waterfront fire station built in 1890 following the Great Fire. (Photo)

Pier 54/Ivar's Acres of Clams Boats in the Mosquito Fleet once moored here at Galbraith Dock. In 1938 Ivar Haglund started his first restaurant and an aquarium here. (Photo)

Miike Maru In 1896 the arrival of the *Miike Maru* with a cargo of tea heralded the first regular shipping service from the Orient as well as the birth of Seattle as an international port.

Railroads Today there are two main railroad tracks along the waterfront where once there were as many as eight to ten. For years known as Railroad Avenue, Alaskan Way was once filled with trains that cut off the waterfront from the rest of downtown.

Cargo Handling Piers 56 and 57 show how cargo used to be handled. Railroad tracks on the narrow aprons (the strip between the wharf edge and warehouse) were used for loading and unloading freight through the large sliding doors into the storage areas.

Piers Most piers and transit sheds are artifacts of those days when ships landed cargo on the central waterfront. The transit sheds were specially designed for moving freight by hook and sling, when railroad activity was at its peak. Most are long and narrow with open floors for storage, but each pier has its own distinct character.

Skinner and Eddy The speed demons of World War I, Skinner and Eddy shipyard turned out 75 8,800-ton freighters in an average of fifty-four days each. The yard closed after the war, and during the Depression was the site of Hooverville, a shanty town of down-and-outers. (Photo)

The Nebraska
Skinner and Eddy
Pier 36/Coast Guard Museum of the Northwest

N

Container Terminal

Alaska Ferries

46
48
50
51
52
53
54
55
56
57

Washington Ferries

Washington Street Public Boat Landing
Alaska Square

Flyer Dock

The Idaho
Ye Olde Curiosity Shop
Yesler's Mill
Battle of Seattle
Fire Station No. 5
Ivar's Acres of Clams
Shops/Food/ Harbor Tours
Colman Dock
Grand Trunk Dock
Ballast Island
Budlong's Boathouse
Joshua Green of Puget Sound Navigation Company/City of Seattle
Klondike Gold Rush National Historical Park
Skid Road
U.S. Coast Guard Cutter Bear

Alaskan Way S.
Western Avenue
First Ave. S.
S. King St.
S. Jackson St.
S. Main St.
Columbia St.
Marion St.
Seneca St.
Union St.
S. Washington St.
Yesler Way

Pioneer Square
The Windward